ORACLE APEX 23

CRASH COURSE FOR BEGINNERS

Explore the NO-CODE Platform to
Build Stunning Web Applications

Saad Muavia

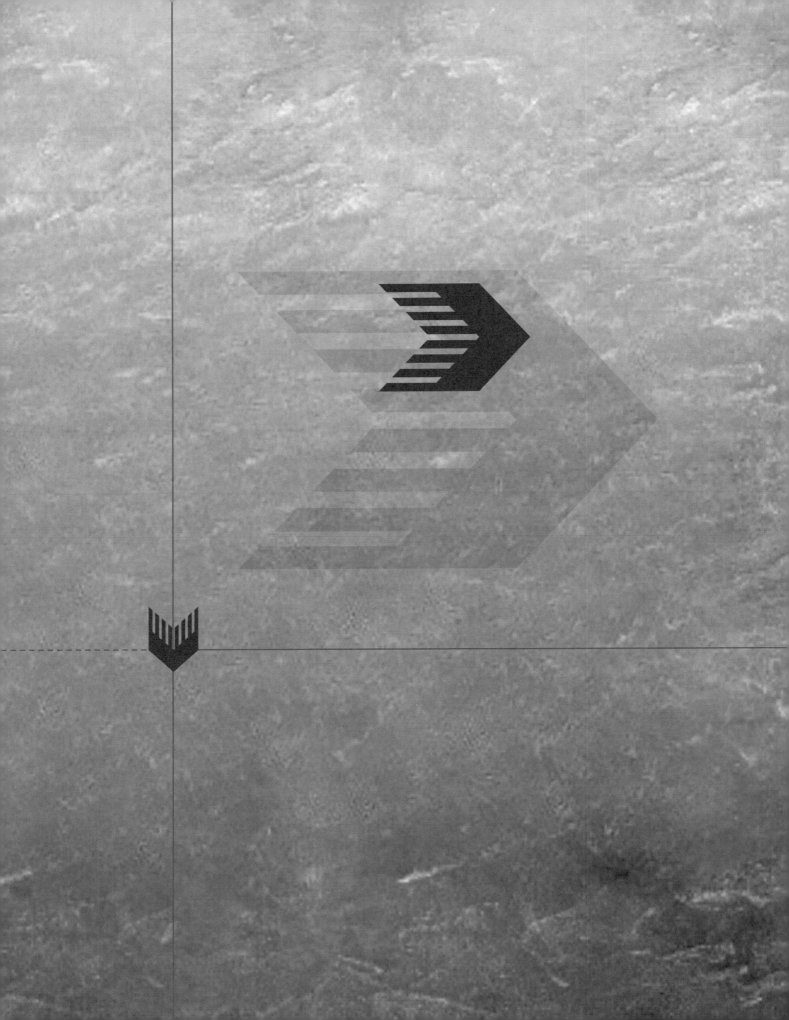

ORACLE APEX 23 CRASH COURSE FOR BEGINNERS

ABOUT THIS BOOK

The objective of this book is to make you an enterprise-grade web application developer in a short span of time using Oracle Application Express (APEX). Oracle APEX is a low-code development platform that allows developers to build scalable, secure, and data-driven web applications quickly. APEX is built on top of the Oracle Database and allows developers to create applications using SQL, PL/SQL, and other Oracle technologies. APEX provides an intuitive web-based interface for developers to design, develop, and deploy applications with ease. The platform offers a wide range of pre-built components such as charts, forms, calendars, and grids, which developers can use to create responsive and modern web applications. With APEX, developers can leverage the power of Oracle Database's security and performance features. APEX also offers tight integration with Oracle Cloud Infrastructure, enabling developers to easily deploy applications to the cloud.

Oracle Application Express (APEX) offers several advantages that make it a popular low-code development platform for building data-driven web applications. Some of the key advantages of APEX include:

Low-code development: APEX provides a user-friendly interface and pre-built components that simplify the application development process, allowing developers to build applications quickly without having to write a lot of code.

Scalability: APEX is built on top of Oracle Database, which provides a robust and scalable platform for managing large amounts of data. Applications built with APEX can easily scale to meet growing business needs.

Security: APEX leverages the security features of Oracle Database, including user authentication and role-based access control, to provide a secure platform for building and deploying applications.

Integration with Oracle technologies: APEX integrates seamlessly with other Oracle technologies, such as Oracle Cloud Infrastructure and Oracle Autonomous Database, enabling developers to leverage these technologies to build and deploy applications in the cloud.

Responsive design: APEX offers a wide range of responsive design templates and components that make it easy to build modern and mobile-friendly web applications.

In summary, APEX provides a powerful and flexible platform for building enterprise-grade web applications quickly and efficiently, with features such as low-code development, scalability, security, integration with Oracle technologies, and responsive design. And this book is rolled out to provide you with a solid foundation of building such applications and teach you the art of web application development.

- Sa'ad Muavia
Author
oratech69@gmail.com

SCAN THE QR CODE
TO DOWNLOAD THE BOOK CODE

AUTHOR

I'm Saad Muavia, an IT enthusiast, author, blogger, and YouTuber. My experiences have sparked a passion in me to expose my skills to everyone. I want to do what I can to bring more diversity into tech and prove to young people that anyone can get into the industry and be successful with a little hard work and the right strategy.

 oratech69@gmail.com

 https://www.youtube.com/@TechMining69

TABLE OF CONTENTS

1

INTRODUCTION

Web Applications

A web application is a software program accessed through a web browser, providing interactive services and functionality over the internet. Unlike traditional desktop applications, web apps don't require installation and are hosted on remote servers. They utilize web technologies like HTML, CSS, JavaScript, and backend languages to generate content, process user input, and interact with databases. Web apps are platform-independent, accessible from any device with a browser and internet connection, making them widely used for delivering diverse online services.

Oracle Application Express (APEX)

Oracle Application Express (APEX) is a low-code development framework that enables the creation of web applications quickly and efficiently. It is built on top of the Oracle Database and utilizes SQL, PL/SQL, and web technologies to develop scalable and secure web applications. With its intuitive user interface, APEX allows developers to design, develop, and deploy feature-rich web applications without the need for extensive coding. It offers a range of built-in components, templates, and themes, along with powerful tools for data manipulation, report generation, and user authentication. Oracle APEX empowers developers to rapidly build and deliver robust web applications, making it a popular choice for businesses seeking to accelerate their development processes.

Declarative Development

Oracle Application Express (APEX) stands out as a declarative development platform, allowing developers to create web applications using a visual, drag-and-drop approach. Instead of writing extensive code, APEX enables developers to define application components and their behaviors through intuitive interfaces. This declarative approach simplifies and expedites application development, reducing the need for manual coding. Developers can easily create forms, reports, charts, and other components by configuring settings and properties. APEX handles the underlying technical implementation, allowing developers to focus on the application's functionality and user experience. With its declarative development capabilities, Oracle APEX empowers developers to build robust web applications efficiently and with minimal coding effort.

Customization

In Oracle APEX, customizing wizard-generated pages is a straightforward process that allows developers to tailor the appearance and functionality of their application's pages. After generating pages using APEX wizards, developers have full control over modifying the generated code, templates, and CSS styles to align with their specific requirements. They can add custom validations, modify the layout, incorporate additional components, and implement business logic to enhance the functionality of the pages. With the ability to customize wizard-generated pages, developers can create personalized and visually appealing user interfaces that align perfectly with their application's design and user experience goals.

Responsive Design

Oracle Application Express (APEX) offers robust support for responsive design, enabling developers to create web applications that adapt seamlessly to various screen sizes and devices. With responsive design in APEX, developers can build applications that automatically adjust their layout, content, and functionality based on the user's device, whether it's a desktop, tablet, or smartphone. APEX provides responsive templates and components that ensure optimal usability and readability across different screen resolutions. Developers can leverage responsive grids, breakpoints, and CSS media queries to design dynamic layouts and make their applications fully responsive. By embracing responsive design in Oracle APEX, developers can deliver a consistent and user-friendly experience, regardless of the device being used to access the application.

How This Book Helps

The best way to truly understand a technology is to apply it to real-world challenges. This book takes an engaging approach, guiding beginners through the exploration of Oracle APEX's features without dwelling on the tedious aspects. By developing a practical application throughout the book, readers gain hands-on experience and a deeper understanding of Oracle APEX. Each chapter focuses on a specific area of functionality, providing development techniques to achieve desired outcomes. The book's captivating style not only introduces the technology but also keeps readers engaged and interested until the final exercise.

ORACLE APEX ANATOMY

ORACLE APEX

Oracle APEX is an integral part of an Oracle database. It is a free low-code rapid application development tool that runs inside an Oracle database instance.

WORKSPACE

In Oracle APEX, you can create multiple workspaces to host different types of applications.

APPLICATIONS

Each workspace can hold multiple applications. Database applications created in Oracle APEX comprise two or more pages.

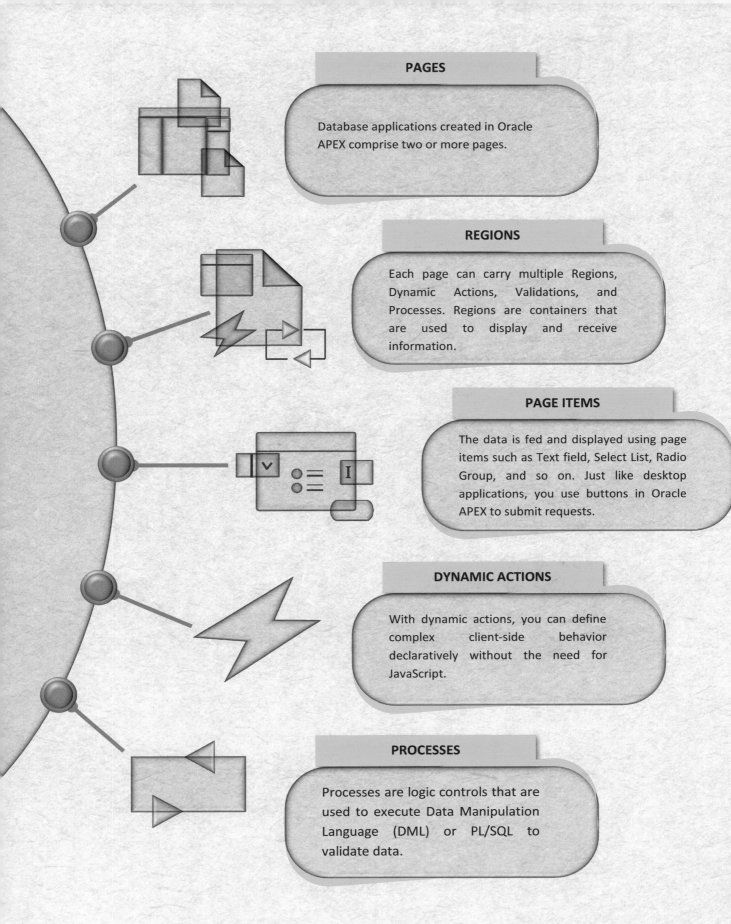

PAGES

Database applications created in Oracle APEX comprise two or more pages.

REGIONS

Each page can carry multiple Regions, Dynamic Actions, Validations, and Processes. Regions are containers that are used to display and receive information.

PAGE ITEMS

The data is fed and displayed using page items such as Text field, Select List, Radio Group, and so on. Just like desktop applications, you use buttons in Oracle APEX to submit requests.

DYNAMIC ACTIONS

With dynamic actions, you can define complex client-side behavior declaratively without the need for JavaScript.

PROCESSES

Processes are logic controls that are used to execute Data Manipulation Language (DML) or PL/SQL to validate data.

WORKSPACE

To access Oracle APEX development environment, users sign in to a shared work area called a Workspace. A workspace is a virtual private container allowing multiple users to work within the same Oracle APEX installation.

You have to create a workspace before you create an application. It is necessary because you have to specify which workspace you want to connect to when you log in. Without this piece of information, you are not allowed to enter Oracle APEX.

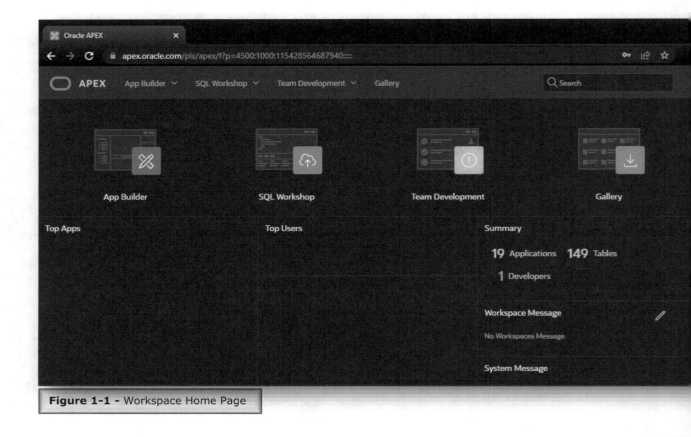

Figure 1-1 - Workspace Home Page

Oracle APEX Workspace serves as a central hub for developers to create, manage, and deploy data-driven applications. It offers a comprehensive set of tools, including a visual application builder, SQL development environment, team development, and a gallery. The Oracle APEX Gallery is a collection of pre-built applications that can be used as a starting point or reference for developing applications in Oracle Application Express. With Oracle APEX Workspace, developers can collaborate, design databases, create interactive web applications, and securely publish them for end-users to access securely.

REQUESTING A FREE WORKSPACE

Follow the instructions mentioned below to get your free workspace:

1. Open your internet browser and type **https://apex.oracle.com/en/** in the address bar to access Oracle APEX site. On the home page, click the **Start for Free Today** button.

2. On the Getting Started page, click the **Free Signup** button.

3. On the Identification wizard screen, enter your first and last names, e-mail address, and the name of the workspace you intend to create – for example, MYWS23. If the workspace name already exists, try a different one. After providing this information, click the **Next** button to proceed to the next wizard step.

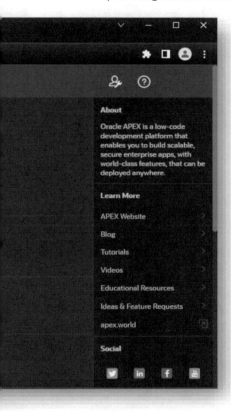

4. On Survey screen, select **Yes** for 'Are you new to Oracle Application Express?' and select appropriate option for the second query. Click **Next** to proceed.

5. On Justification screen provide a justification like, "**I want to evaluate Oracle APEX**" and click **Next**.

6. On the next wizard screen read and accept the agreement terms.

7. Click the **Submit Request** button on the final Confirmation screen. A confirmation box will pop up with the message "You will receive an email to activate your workspace once this request has been approved."

8. Soon after submitting the request, you'll get an e-mail from Oracle carrying your workspace credentials and a button labeled Create Workspace. Take a note of your credentials because you need this information whenever you attempt to access your online Oracle APEX workspace. Click the **Create Workspace** button to complete the approval process. You will be taken to Oracle APEX's website, and after a little while, your request will be approved with the message "*Workspace Successfully Created*."

9. Click the **Continue to Sign In Screen** button.

10. A screen appears requesting to change password. Enter and confirm your password and click the **Apply Changes** button. Write down the password along with the workspace credentials.

11. Here you go! Your Workspace Home Page comes up resembling Figure 1-1.

12. To leave the Oracle APEX environment, click your name (appearing at top-right) and select **Sign Out**.

The App Builder allows you to create dynamic database driven web applications. This is the place where you create and modify your applications and pages. It comprises the following:

Create	Import	Dashboard	Workspace Utilities
This is the option in the App Builder that is used to create new applications.	Used to import an entire Oracle APEX application developed somewhere else, along with related objects.	Presents different metrics about applications in your workspace including: Developer Activity, Page Events, Page Count by Application, and Most Active Pages.	It contains various workspace utilities. The most significant one is Export. Using this utility, you can export application and component metadata to SQL script file format that you can import on the same or another compatible instance of Application Express.

Team Development allows development teams to better manage their Oracle APEX projects by defining milestones, features, to-dos, and bugs. Features, to-dos, and bugs can be associated with specific applications and pages as necessary. Developers can readily configure feedback to allow their end-users to provide comments on applications. The feedback also captures relevant session state details and can be readily converted to a feature, to-do or bug.

Use SQL Workshop to browse your database objects and to run ad-hoc SQL queries. SQL Workshop is designed to allow Application Developers to maintain database objects such as tables, packages, functions, views, and so on. It is beneficial in hosted environments like apex.oracle.com where direct access to underlying schemas is not provided. It has five basic components:

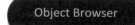

Object Browser

SQL Commands
SQL Scripts

Utilities

RESTful Services

The Object Browser in Oracle APEX is a visual tool for exploring and managing database objects (tables, views, functions, triggers, and so on) within an application, simplifying the process of viewing and modifying object properties and performing related actions.

The *SQL Commands* refer to a feature that allows developers to directly execute SQL statements and queries. This feature enables developers to perform tasks such as retrieving data, updating records, creating database objects, and executing complex SQL operations. You use *SQL Scripts* to upload and execute script files.

It contains a variety of tools and functionalities that assist developers in managing and enhancing their applications. Some of the common options found in the Utilities menu include: Query Builder, Data Workshop, Generate DDL, Schema Comparison, and more.

In Oracle APEX, RESTful Services refer to a feature that enables developers to create and manage RESTful web services within their applications. RESTful services allow applications to expose data and functionality in a standardized and web-friendly manner, making it easier to integrate with external systems.

The Gallery contains starter apps that are a suite of business productivity applications, easily installed with only a few clicks. These solutions can be readily used as production applications to improve business processes.

APPLICATIONS

An application in Oracle APEX is a web-based solution that combines pages, navigation, shared components, data management, business logic, security, and user interface customization to fulfill a specific business or user requirement. It provides a platform for rapid application development with minimal coding and leverages the power of an Oracle database for data storage and retrieval.

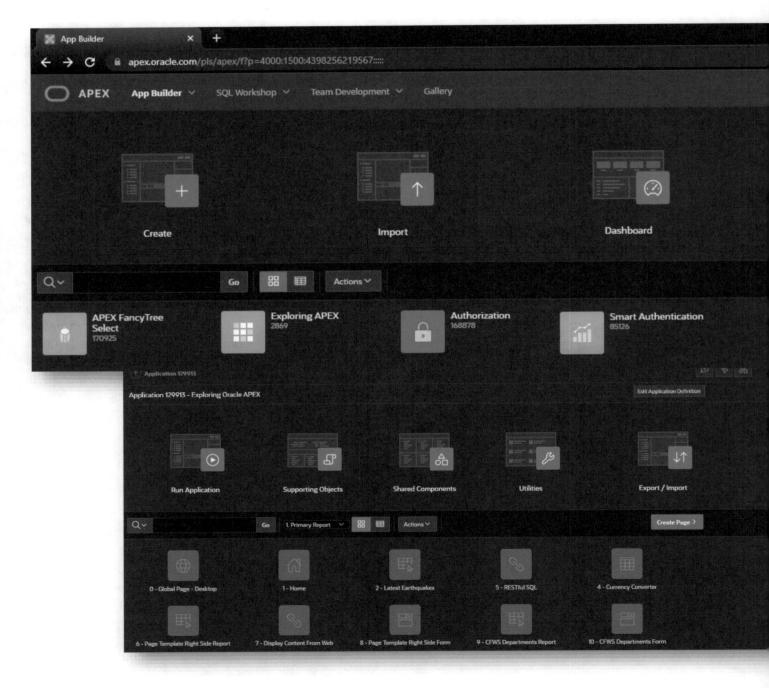

Applications in Oracle APEX are created using App Builder and each application consists of one or more pages that are linked together via a navigation menu, buttons, or hypertext links. The App Builder home page (Figure 1-2) displays all installed applications in the current Oracle APEX instance.

When a developer selects an application to edit, the Application home page (Figure 1-3) appears. Using the Application home page you can modify, copy, delete, run, or import applications.

Figure 1-2 – App Builder

Figure 1-3 – Application Home Page

The Create button and icon on the App Builder page launches the Create Application wizard comprising the following options:

New Application

By utilizing this feature, you have the ability to generate a comprehensive application that relies on database tables. Within this application, you can incorporate a diverse range of pages, encompassing components such as reports, input forms, charts, maps, calendars, cards, master-detail forms, interactive grids, and more. Moreover, this feature enables the addition of application-level functionalities, including an about page, role-based user authentication, end-user activity reports, configuration options to enable or disable specific features, a feedback mechanism for gathering user comments, and the ability for end users to select their preferred theme style. These applications seamlessly interact with a backend Oracle database to handle data storage and retrieval operations.

From a File

This option empowers you to create an application by importing data from a CSV, XLSX, XML, or JSON file. When you initiate the Create Application Wizard and opt for this choice, the Load Data Wizard emerges, allowing you to load a CSV, XLSX, XML, or JSON file. Oracle APEX takes charge by generating a fresh table based on the specifications provided within the selected file, and subsequently populates it with the accompanying data. Additionally, you have the flexibility to Copy and Paste column-delimited data as an alternative approach. Once the data is successfully loaded into the database table, the wizard proceeds to create a set of application pages based on the newly formed table.

Starter Apps

Starter Apps comprise a collection of business productivity and sample applications that can be effortlessly installed with minimal effort. These applications are comprehensive and ready-to-use solutions, purposefully created to deliver practical functionality. Starter apps can be swiftly installed, executed, and uninstalled as needed. On the other hand, applications falling under the Sample Apps category showcase specific functionalities and serve as invaluable developer references, providing guidance on effectively utilizing particular features.

PAGES

In Oracle Application Express, a page is a fundamental element of an application's user interface. It consists of regions, items, buttons, and other components that facilitate data presentation, user interaction, and navigation.

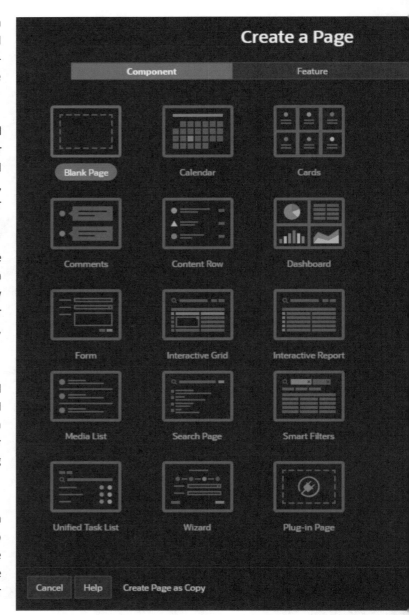

Blank Page A blank page is a page that provides a clean and empty canvas for developers to design and customize from scratch. It is a blank slate without any pre-defined regions or components, allowing developers to have complete control over the layout and content of the page.

Calendar a calendar page refers to a specialized page template designed to display and manage events or appointments in a calendar format. It provides a visual representation of time-based data, allowing users to view, create, edit, and interact with events within a calendar interface.

Form A form page is a user interface component that allows users to view and manipulate data stored in an Oracle database. It provides a convenient way to create, update, and delete records within a table or multiple tables. It comprises input fields, buttons, validations, and automatic DML process.

Interactive Grid an Interactive Grid page is a powerful component that provides a highly interactive and customizable way to view, edit, and manipulate data from one or more database tables. It offers advanced features for data entry, sorting, filtering, aggregating, and manipulating data directly within the grid.

Interactive Report An Interactive Report is a component that provides a powerful and flexible way to display, explore, and analyze data from one or more database tables. It allows users to interactively manipulate and customize the report's output based on their preferences and requirements.

Smart Filters A smart filters page features single search field at the top of the page and a search results report (classic report, cards, map, or calendar). While a Smart Filter behaves similarly to faceted search, it features a more space efficient layout.

Chart   A Chart page is a component that allows you to visualize data in the form of interactive charts and graphs. It provides a powerful way to present data in a visually appealing manner, enabling users to gain insights and make informed decisions.

Classic Report   A Classic Report page is a component that allows you to display and present data in a tabular format. It provides a flexible and customizable way to present data from one or more database tables or SQL queries.

Data Loading   A Data Loading page is a component that facilitates the bulk loading or importing of data into the application from external sources. It provides a user-friendly interface to upload files and process the data within those files, populating the database tables or APEX collections.

Faceted Search   Faceted search in Oracle APEX refers to a search and filtering technique that allows users to explore and narrow down search results based on multiple facets or attributes associated with the data. It provides a user-friendly and interactive way to refine search queries and navigate through large datasets.

Map   A Map page is a component that allows you to visualize and interact with geographical data on an interactive map. It enables you to display markers, regions, and other geographic elements based on the data from your database.

Master Detail   A Master-Detail page is a component that allows you to display and interact with related data from two or more database tables or views. It provides a way to present a master record and its associated detail records in a single page, facilitating data entry, editing, and navigation.

Timeline   Creates a page with a Timeline region for displaying a series of events. The Timeline region can be used to showcase the history of a given widget, recent updates, or new interactions within an application.

Tree   a Tree page is a component that allows you to display hierarchical data in a tree-like structure. It provides a visual representation of parent-child relationships, allowing users to navigate and interact with the hierarchical data.

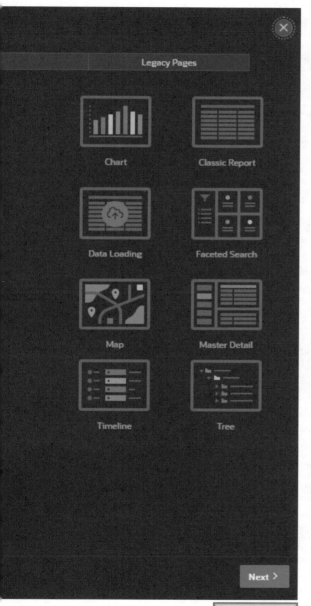

Figure 1-4

Push Notifications Push notifications refer to the capability of sending real-time notifications or messages to users' devices or web browsers. With push notifications, you can deliver important updates, alerts, or reminders directly to users, even when they are not actively using your application.

About Page Include an About this Application page which features a description field that describes the application, includes the application version, and a count of the number of pages.

Access Control An Access Control page is a component used for managing user access and permissions within your application. It provides a user interface for administrators or developers to define and control who can perform specific actions or access certain parts of the application.

Email Reporting Include numerous reports on emails queued from this application, emails sent, and errors sending emails.

Feedback A Feedback page is a component that allows users to provide feedback, suggestions, or report issues about the application. It serves as a communication channel between users and the application's administrators or developers.

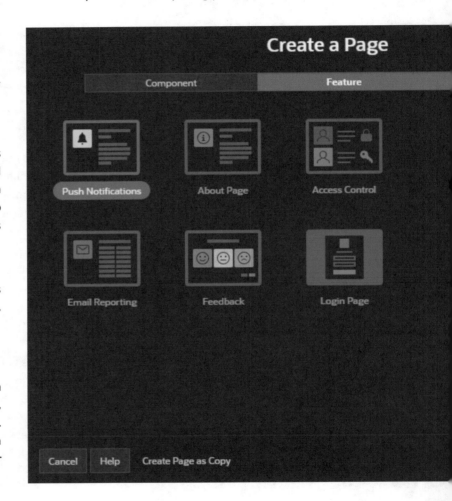

Login Page A Login page is a key component that provides a secure authentication mechanism for users to access an application. It presents a user interface where users can enter their credentials (username and password) to authenticate and gain access to the protected areas of the application.

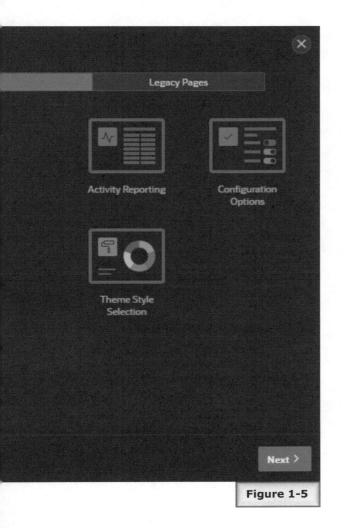

Figure 1-5

Activity Reporting It provides a variety of reports on end user activity, enabling you to identify the most active users, frequently accessed pages, page performance, and any raised errors. This comprehensive insight allows you to gain a deeper understanding of how your application is being utilized and pinpoint areas that can be enhanced for improved performance.

Configuration Options It allows administrators to toggle specific functionality on or off. This capability proves valuable when selecting features that require further development before being accessible to end users. Furthermore, you can extend this functionality to encompass application-specific features. By defining additional build options and associating them with particular functionalities across the application, developers can include them in the configuration settings accessible to administrators.

Theme Style Selection It empowers administrators to set a default color scheme (theme style) for the entire application. Moreover, administrators have the option to permit end users to select their preferred theme style. To do this, end users can access the Customize button located at the bottom of the home page and choose from the available theme styles. For instance, users with visual impairments may opt for the Vista theme style due to its significantly higher color contrast.

A region is a fundamental building block used to organize and display content on a page and page items are variables or placeholders that store user input, session state, or other data on a specific page.

Region A region is a fundamental building block used to organize and display content on a page. A region represents a distinct section of the page and can contain various types of content and components. It acts as a container for items, reports, charts, and other APEX components, allowing developers to organize and present data in a structured manner.

Regions in APEX provide a way to control the layout and presentation of data on a page. They help in creating a structured user interface by dividing the page into logical sections. APEX offers several pre-built region types, such as Static Content Region, Interactive Report Region, Interactive Grid Region, Form Region, Chart Region and more, each designed to serve specific purposes.

Developers can add, remove, and rearrange regions on a page to create the desired layout and functionality. Each region type comes with specific attributes and customization options to tailor the appearance and behavior according to the application's requirements.

Regions play a significant role in organizing and presenting data in APEX applications, making the development process more efficient and enabling users to have a better experience when interacting with the application's content.

In Oracle APEX, an application component can either be created as a page or as a region. For example, you can create a new Form page, or add a Form Region to an existing page. Both Form Page and Form Region are used to display and edit data from a single database table, but they have different purposes and implementations. The main difference between a Form Page and a Form Region in Oracle APEX is that a Form Page is a complete and standalone page specifically designed for data manipulation on a single table, while a Form Region is a modular component that can be added to any page to provide data entry and editing capabilities within a more complex user interface. The choice between using a form page or a form region depends on the specific requirements and design of the application.

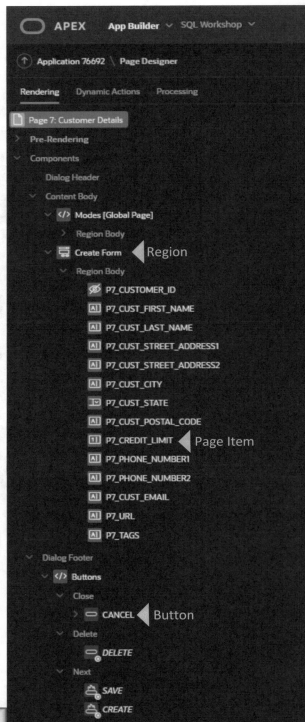

Figure 1-6

Page Items Page items are variables or placeholders that store user input, session state, or other data on a specific page. They are a fundamental component used to capture and manage data in APEX applications. Page items are associated with form elements, such as text fields, select lists, checkboxes, and date pickers, allowing users to input or select data that can be processed and used by the application.

Page items can be classified into the following types:

1. **Text Items**: Text items are used to capture and store single-line text input from users. They are commonly used for capturing names, addresses, comments, and other textual data.

2. **Text Area Items**: Text area items are used for capturing multi-line text input, such as longer comments or descriptions.

3. **Select List Items**: Select list items, also known as drop-down lists, allow users to choose a single value from a predefined list of options.

4. **Radio Group Items**: Radio group items present users with a list of choices, and they can select only one option from the list.

5. **Checkbox Items**: Checkbox items are used for binary choices where users can select or deselect an option.

6. **Date Picker Items**: Date picker items enable users to select a date using a calendar interface.

7. **File Browse Items**: File browse items allow users to upload files from their local machine to the application.

Page items are defined and managed within the APEX application's Page Designer. Each page item is associated with a unique name, which is used to reference and manipulate its value during page processing. The name of a page item is preceded by the letter P followed by the page number. For example, P7_CUSTOMER_ID represents customer ID item on page 7. Each item has its own specific properties that affect the display of items on a page. For example, these properties can impact where a label displays, how large an item is, and if the item displays next to or below the previous item.

Buttons In Oracle APEX, buttons are interactive components used to trigger specific actions or processes within an application. Buttons allow users to perform various tasks, such as submitting a form, navigating to another page, executing a PL/SQL process, or invoking a dynamic action.

APEX provides several types of buttons, each with its unique behavior and purpose:

1. **Submit Button**: A submit button is often associated with a form and is used to submit the form data to the server for processing. When a user clicks a submit button, the form's data is sent to the server, and any associated processes or validations are executed.

2. **Reset Button**: A reset button is used to reset the values of form items back to their initial state. When clicked, it clears the form fields and restores them to their default or initial values.

3. **Navigation Button**: Navigation buttons are used to navigate to another page within the application or to external URLs. They allow users to move between different sections or pages of the application.

4. **Report Button**: Report buttons are typically used in interactive reports or grid regions to perform actions related to the displayed data, such as calling an input form page.

5. **Custom Button**: Custom buttons are versatile and can be used for various purposes. Developers can define custom JavaScript code or PL/SQL processes to execute when the button is clicked.

6. **Modal Dialog Close Button**: Modal dialog close buttons are used to close modal dialogs (pop-up windows) when clicked by the user.

Developers can customize button styles and appearance using CSS classes and themes to match the application's design and branding. Additionally, buttons can be conditionally displayed or hidden based on certain criteria using APEX expressions, enabling a dynamic user interface that adapts to the user's actions or the data displayed.

The page designer is a powerful and user-friendly visual development environment that allows developers to design and customize the pages of their APEX applications. It provides a graphical interface for creating, modifying, and managing pages, regions, items, and other components within an application.

The Tree pane is displayed on the left side in the Page Designer. It contains regions, items, buttons, application logic (such as computations and processes), dynamic actions, branches, and shared components as nodes on a tree. It comprises four tabs.

The Rendering tab displays regions, page items, page buttons, and application logic as nodes in a tree, organized by their processing order during page rendering. The rendering process is divided into three stages: Pre-Rendering, Components Rendering, and Post-Rendering. In the Pre-Rendering stage, preliminary computations take place. The Components Rendering stage handles regions and their components, while the Post-Rendering stage performs computations after the page is rendered.

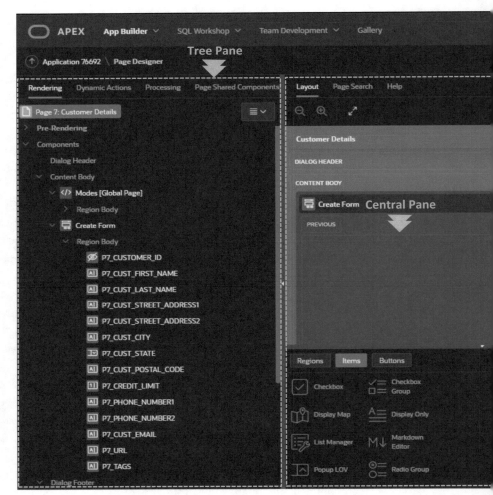

Dynamic Actions are a powerful and declarative way to create interactive and responsive behavior in APEX applications without the need for custom JavaScript code. They allow developers to define actions and conditions based on user interactions or changes in the application, triggering various behaviors and updates in real-time.

The Processing tab allows you to define the application logic, including validations, processes, and branches. *Validations* are server-side checks to ensure the accuracy and consistency of data submitted before saving it to the database. *Processes* are used for executing Data Manipulation Language (DML) or PL/SQL actions. *Branches* help determine the user's navigation flow within the application.

On the Page Shared Components tab, you can view shared components associated with the page. This list is automatically populated when shared components are used on the page.

At the top of the page, you will find the Toolbar, which offers a range of tools for various actions. These include options to search for a page, lock or unlock a page, undo or redo action, save and run the page, and more. When you hover your cursor over an active option, a tooltip provides a brief description of its function. Within the Utilities menu, there is a "Delete" option that allows you to permanently remove the currently displayed page in the Page Designer from the application, along with all its associated components.

The toolbar also includes a lock icon to indicate the page's locking status. An open padlock signifies an unlocked page, while a locked padlock indicates that the page is currently locked. This locking feature is helpful for preventing conflicts during application development, as it restricts other developers from making edits to a locked page. The locked status is displayed not only in Page Designer but also on the Application home page, ensuring clear visibility of the page's locking state.

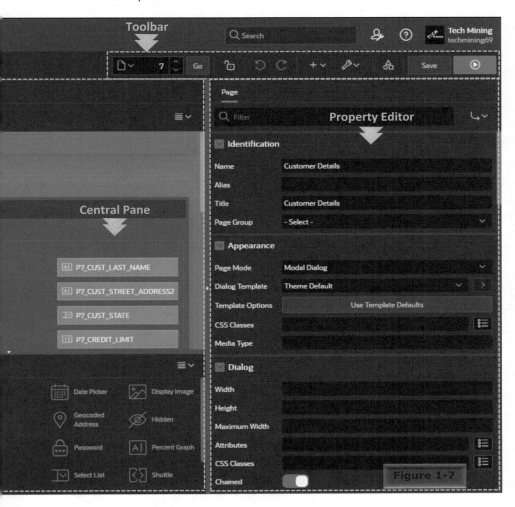

Figure 1-7

The Property Editor is a user interface component that allows developers to manage and configure various properties of different components within an APEX application. It provides a centralized and efficient way to customize the behavior and appearance of application elements, such as pages, regions, items, buttons, charts, and more. For example, you can use the Property Editor to set page-level properties like the page title, template, security settings, and other attributes that affect the overall behavior of the page. For each region on a page, the Property Editor allows you to modify properties like the region title, region template, source SQL query or PL/SQL code, and other region-specific settings. The same applies to all page components, such as items, buttons, and charts. The Property Editor reduces the need for manual coding and allows developers to visually configure and fine-tune the behavior of their application elements efficiently.

The Page Designer's Central pane is divided into two sections. The upper section comprises three tabs: Layout, Page Search, and Help. The lower section, known as the Gallery, is associated with the Layout tab. The Layout tab offers a visual representation of the page, showing its regions, items, and buttons. To add new regions, items, or buttons to the page, you can select them from the Gallery located at the bottom of the page. For a comprehensive search of all page metadata, including regions, items, buttons, dynamic actions, and columns, you can utilize the Page Search feature.

Additionally, the Help tab in the central pane provides assistance regarding the properties available in the Property Editor. Whenever you select a property in the Property Editor, you can access relevant help text by clicking on the Help tab. This allows you to understand the purpose and functionality of the selected property. As you navigate between different properties in the Property Editor, the Help tab dynamically updates and displays the corresponding help text for the currently selected property.

DYNAMIC ACTIONS

Dynamic Actions are a powerful declarative way to define client-side behavior in web applications. They allow developers to create interactive and responsive user interfaces without the need for custom JavaScript code. With Dynamic Actions, you can specify actions that should occur when certain events happen on the client-side, such as button clicks, item changes, page load, and more.

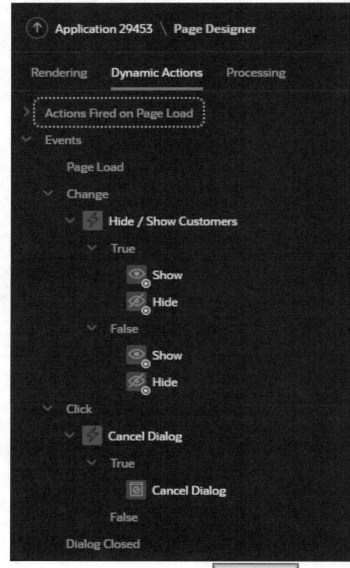

Here's an overview of how Dynamic Actions work:

1. **Event**: A Dynamic Action is triggered by a specific event that occurs on a page. Events can include things like button clicks, item value changes, page load, page unload, and more.

2. **Selection**: You select the element (e.g., button, item, region) that should trigger the Dynamic Action when the specified event occurs. For example, you might choose a particular button, or an item with a specific ID.

3. **Condition (Optional)**: You can set conditions to control when the Dynamic Action should execute. For instance, you might want the action to occur only if a certain item has a specific value or meets certain criteria.

4. **True and False Actions**: For each Dynamic Action, you define the actions that should happen when the condition evaluates to true (True Actions) and optionally when it evaluates to false (False Actions). These actions can be a wide range of things, such as showing/hiding page elements, setting item values, executing PL/SQL code, performing AJAX requests, and more.

5. **Client-side Processing**: Dynamic Actions execute on the client-side to provide an interactive user experience without the need for server round-trips.

Dynamic Actions make it easier for developers to create dynamic and interactive web applications without writing custom JavaScript code. They are an essential part of Oracle APEX's declarative development approach and allow developers to focus on application logic and behavior rather than low-level implementation details.

Figure 1-8

PROCESSING

Processes are units of server-side logic that are executed when a specific event occurs during the processing of a page request. Processes allow developers to implement custom business logic, perform database operations, and execute server-side actions in response to user interactions or other events in an APEX application.

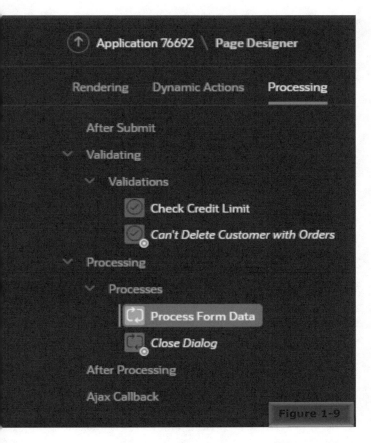

Figure 1-9

There are several types of processes in APEX:

1. Page Processes: These processes are associated with a specific page in the application and are executed during the processing of that page. Page processes can be further categorized into:

    a. Before Header: Processes executed before the page is rendered, typically used for setting initial values or doing some preparatory work.

    b. Before Regions: Processes executed before rendering the regions on the page, useful for any logic that needs to be executed before displaying regions.

    c. After Submit: Processes executed after the page is submitted, typically used for processing user input or performing database operations.

    d. Processing: Processes executed during the processing phase of page submission, commonly used for more complex server-side actions.

    e. After Processing: Processes executed after the page is processed, often used for finalizing actions or cleanup.

2. Branch Processes: These processes define conditions for navigation from one page to another based on certain criteria. They determine which page to navigate to next in the application flow.

3. Computations: Computations are processes that calculate and set the value of page items or application-level variables.

4. Validations: Validation processes check user input or specific conditions to ensure that the data meets the required criteria before proceeding further.

5. Automatic Row Processing (DML): These processes are automatically generated for Interactive Grids and input forms and handle database operations for each row in the grid or data entered in the input form.

6. PL/SQL Code: Developers can create custom processes that execute PL/SQL code to perform complex business logic or database operations.

Shared components are pre-built and reusable elements that can be utilized across multiple pages or applications. Shared components in Oracle APEX are created once and can be used in various parts of your application or even across multiple applications within the same workspace. Here are some of the key shared components:

Navigation Menu: A navigation menu is a shared component that provides a consistent menu structure for your application. It allows you to define a hierarchical menu with links to different pages and reports.

Theme and Template: A theme defines the look and feel of your application, including color schemes, fonts, and styling. A template determines the layout and structure of your pages. Both themes and templates are shared components that can be applied across multiple pages.

Authentication and Authorization: Components like authentication schemes and authorization schemes can be shared to enforce consistent security policies across the application.

REST Data Sources: These options are used to connect to web services, RESTful APIs, or other web resources that provide data in a structured format (e.g., JSON, XML, or CSV). With these options, you can define the URL of the web service, specify request parameters, and configure authentication if required. Once the REST data source is set up, you can use it to fetch data from the external web service and integrate that data into your APEX application.

Progressive Web App (PWA): It is a type of web application that incorporates modern web technologies to provide a native app-like experience to users. PWAs are designed to work offline, load quickly, and be responsive across different devices. They offer features such as push notifications, offline caching, and the ability to add the app to the device's home screen, similar to native mobile apps.

Application Access Control: It refers to the management and enforcement of security policies that control user access to different parts of an APEX application. Access Control requires that developers define application users and roles. Since roles are applied to users, you must create roles before adding users. You can assign users to one or more roles.

List of Values (LOV): An LOV is a shared component that defines a list of predefined values, which can be used to populate select lists, radio groups, or popup LOVs on various pages.

Plug-ins: These are reusable components that extend the functionality of your APEX applications. They are custom-built or pre-packaged modules that developers can integrate seamlessly into their applications to add new features, interactions, and visualizations that may not be available out-of-the-box in APEX.

Shortcuts: Use Shortcuts to write frequently used code once and then reference it in many places within your application. For example, you create a shortcut that displays a confirmation message before deleting a record. Since this shortcut is created in Shared Components, all application pages can utilize it to present the same confirmation message whenever a record is deleted.

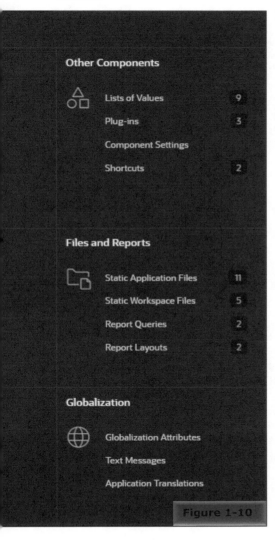

Figure 1-10

Static Application/Workspace Files: These are shared components used to store and manage static files that are associated with an APEX application. Static files are non-dynamic resources such as JavaScript files, CSS files, images, fonts, and other files that are not generated or processed by APEX at runtime. Instead, they are served directly to the client's web browser, providing additional resources to enhance the user interface and functionality of the application. An application file can be referenced from a specific application only, whereas a workspace file can be accessed by any application in the workspace.

Report Queries: A report query is a printable document that can be seamlessly integrated into an application through buttons, list items, branches, or other navigational components that support URL targets. This type of query relies on a standard SQL query and offers several download options, including PDF, Word (RTF based), Excel Spreadsheet (HTML based), and HTML formats. The presentation layout of a report query is customizable using RTF templates. It's important to note that for this feature to function, your application must utilize a remote print server.

Report Layouts: Use Report Layouts in conjunction with a report query to render data in a printer-friendly format, such as PDF, Word or Excel. A report layout can be designed using the Template Builder Word plug-in and uploaded as a file of type RTF or XSL-FO. For this, your application must utilize a remote print server, such as Oracle BI Publisher. Besides standard configuration, Oracle BI Publisher has Word Template Plug-in to create RTF based report layouts, which provides greater control over every aspect of your report and allows you to add complex control breaks, logos, charts, and pagination control. Invoices, ledgers, and financial statements are some examples that you can create with this option.

Application Translations: Applications can be translated into multiple languages, creating separate translated versions. Each translation requires a mapping specifying the target language and translated application ID. The translatable text is stored in a translation repository, exported to XLIFF for translation, and uploaded back to the repository. Translated applications are published from the repository. Synchronization is needed when the primary application is modified after the translated version is published.

WHAT YOU LEARNED

▶ Got an overview of web applications, Oracle APEX, declarative development, and responsive design.

    ▶ Went through the Oracle APEX anatomy.

        ▶ Learned about workspace and created a free workspace for subsequent exercises.

        ▶ Got conceptual knowledge of Oracle APEX applications and different types of application pages.

    ▶ You also learned about page components, such as regions, page items, and buttons.

▶ You were also briefed on page designer, dynamic actions, processes, and shared components.

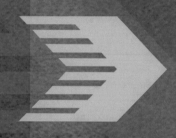

GETTING STARTED

2

CREATE APPLICATION

After familiarizing yourself with the essential foundational principles of Oracle APEX, it's time to embark on the exciting journey! Proceed with the instructions provided in this section to craft the fundamental structure of your first Oracle APEX application.

1. If you have logged out, sign back into the Oracle APEX development environment by typing the URL https://apex.oracle.com/pls/apex/f?p=4550 in your browser's address bar.

Figure 2-1

2. In the Sign In form, enter the credential comprising your Workspace, Username (your e-mail address), and Password you provided in the "Requesting a Free Workspace" section in the previous chapter and hit the Sign In button. You'll see your workspace home page.

3. On your workspace home page, click on the App Builder icon. As a developer, you will utilize App Builder to design and oversee applications and their respective pages. The App Builder's main page exhibits all applications within the existing Oracle Application Express workspace. Upon selecting an application for editing, the Application home page will be presented, enabling you to execute tasks such as running, editing, importing, exporting, copying, or deleting applications.

Figure 2-2

4. On the App Builder page, click the Create icon (or click the Create button) to create a new application.

Figure 2-3

Figure 2-5

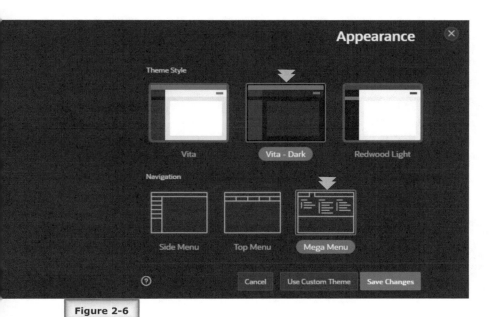

Figure 2-6

Figure 2-7

5. On the first wizard screen, select the Use Create App Wizard option. This selection will generate a fresh database application that includes multiple pages based on existing database tables. A database application consists of interconnected pages, facilitated by navigation menus, tabs, buttons, or hypertext links. These application pages share a unified session state and authentication.

6. Enter a name for the application – for example, Exploring APEX. You can change the application icon by clicking the default icon appearing to the left of the application name. In the Appearance section, click the Set Appearance icon.

7. On the Appearance page, select Vita-Dark for Theme Style, and Mega Menu for Navigation. In Oracle APEX, you can modify a database application's interface using themes and theme styles. The Mega Menu is a collapsible floating panel displaying all navigation items at once, accessible through a menu icon in the header. It enhances user experience by providing easy access to all navigation items simultaneously. You can change these two options any time through Shared Components | Application Definition | User Interface | Attributes and Navigation Menu options. Save the changes.

8. The Pages section enables you to include pages in your initial application. By default, the App Builder process generates a Home page along with a few pages (Login and Global – not visible in this list) for your application. You can utilize the Add Page option to create additional pages.

9. In the Features section, click Check All to select all listed features for the application. The Features section provides application-level functionality and can only be added once per application.

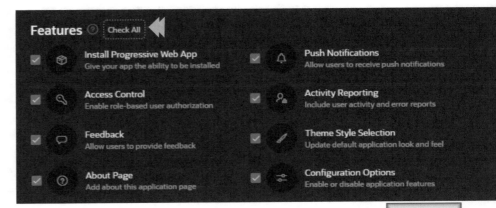

Figure 2-8

Progressive Web App

The Progressive Web App (PWA) technology transforms your APEX application that looks and feels like a native desktop application. PWAs can work offline, send push notifications, and provide an overall smoother user experience, similar to native mobile applications. When you choose this feature, a new navigation bar entry labeled Install App is displayed in your application's navigation bar.

Access Control

Implement role-based user authentication in your application, where users are categorized as Administrators, Contributors, or Readers. By doing so, you can easily configure distinct access levels for different roles across various components in your application, including pages, menu entries, regions, columns, items, buttons, and more.

Feedback

Implements a system that allows end users to submit general comments to application administrators and developers. By establishing this straightforward feedback loop, communication between the user community and application owners is improved, resulting in significantly enhanced end user satisfaction.

About Page

Includes an about this application page which features a description of the application, the application version, and a page count.

Push Notifications

Push notifications are short messages that can be sent to users' devices including mobile and desktop instantly even when the application is not open or the device is not actively in use. These notifications can enhance user experience by providing updates alerts and reminders allowing users to stay informed and connected to your Apex application at all time.

Activity Reporting

Incorporate a variety of reports on end user activity within your application. These reports will provide valuable insights, including identifying the most active users, the frequently accessed pages, page performance metrics, and any raised errors.

Theme Style Selection

Using this feature, administrators can choose a default color scheme (theme style) for the application. They can also enable or disable the ability for end users to select their own theme style from Shared Components. For instance, users with visual impairment may opt for the Vista theme style, which offers a much higher color contrast.

Configuration Options

Enables application administrators to enable or disable specific functionality within the application. This feature is useful for application segments that need additional development effort before they can be used by end users.

Figure 2-9

10. In the Settings section, keep all the default values as they are. The Application ID is a unique identifier used to identify your application. If necessary, you can provide a different non-existent number for your application. The Schema drop-down list displays the name of the schema you are currently connected to. This schema stores the database objects (tables, sequences, triggers, etc.) for your application. Oracle APEX offers various predefined authentication mechanisms, including a built-in authentication framework and a customizable custom framework. In the default Oracle APEX Accounts authentication scheme, users are managed and maintained within the Oracle APEX repository. Click the Create Application button to complete the process.

A After creating the application, you will be landed on the following page, which is the application home page. It displays the application's ID (247166) and its name (Exploring APEX). Use this page to run, edit, import, export, copy, or delete an application.

B To modify properties of the application (e.g., application name or menu position), click the Edit Application Definition button. In the Edit Application Definition interface, you'll find a small question mark icon next to each property. Click it to learn more about any unfamiliar property.

C Clicking the Run Application icon allows you to execute the application. Use the Shared Components option to access the Shared Components page. Export/Import options let you transfer and get an application, respectively.

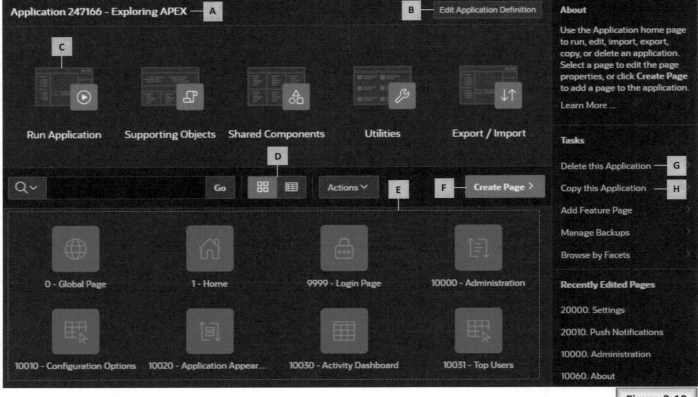

Figure 2-10

D These two buttons, View Icons and View Report, offer different views of this interface. The screenshot above shows the iconic view.

E The application is created with some default pages, including Page 0 Global Page, Page 1 Home, and Page 9999 Login Page.

F In subsequent chapters, you will use this Create Page button to generate new application pages.

G You can delete an application using the Delete this Application link.

H You can create a copy of the application with the Copy this Application link. The link makes an exact copy of the application under a different ID.

11. On the application home page, click Run Application (C).

I The application login page, created by the App Builder, will appear in a new tab. Type the same username (your e-mail ID) and the password you entered earlier to access the development environment and click the Sign In button.

J The new browser window will show the Home page of your application. This page is also created by the App Builder.

K This is the application's mega menu. Currently it has two entries. Options are added to this menu when you add new pages to the application.

L This is the navigation bar. When users click the Install App option, the application is opened in a standalone window. Using the feedback icon (next to Install App) you can leave a comment. And you exit the application using the Sign Out option under your id.

Figure 2-11

M The Developer Toolbar is a useful tool that appears at the bottom of the page when you run an application in the development environment. It provides developers and administrators with quick access to various development-related features and options while working on an application.

The toolbar allows you to access session information like session ID and user ID, aiding in debugging and monitoring. It also enables developers to enable/disable debugging for the current session, providing helpful debug messages and error details for issue identification and troubleshooting.

The App option takes you to the application home page, where you can select a different page to work on. The Page option takes you to the page designer interface where you can modify the current page. For example, if you click this option in the current scenario, you will see Page 1 in the page designer.

Theme Roller empowers developers to effortlessly alter the visual aspects of an application. As a dynamic CSS editor, it allows users to swiftly adjust colors, incorporate rounded corners to regions, and define various properties of their applications, all without requiring any manual coding.

CREATE FIRST PAGE

Once you have set up the basic structure of your application, the next step involves adding pages to it. To get acquainted with the process, begin by adding a blank page. Once the page is created, you will proceed to include a region and page items in it.

1. On the application home page, click the Create Page button - see point D in figure 2-10.

2. On the first wizard screen, click on the first Blank Page option.

3. Fill in the Page Definition wizard screen as shown here and click the Create Page button.

First, you enter a non-existent number for the page. Every page in your application must have a unique number. Then, you provide a name for your page.

The Page Mode property determines the page's display behavior in Oracle APEX. By default, newly created pages are set to Normal mode. In Normal mode, when you call the page, it replaces the existing page displayed in the browser. In contrast, a Modal Dialog page is an independent page that appears on top of its calling page, restricting users from performing other actions until it is closed. Modal Dialog pages can only be displayed on top of another page.

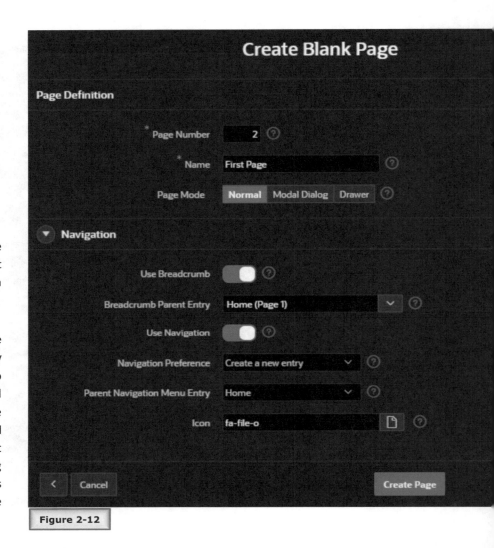

Figure 2-12

A breadcrumb is a sequential list of links that represents the user's location within the application's hierarchy. It allows users to easily navigate back to any previous level by clicking on a specific breadcrumb link. In this application, breadcrumbs are utilized as a secondary level of navigation at the top of each page. To establish the hierarchical structure, you designated the "Home" menu entry as the Parent Entry for this page.

When the Use Navigation option is turned on, the remaining three options under it become visible. You use this option to enable navigation for this page. You select how you want this page to be integrated into the Navigation Menu. By selecting the Create a new entry, you will be able to navigate to the new page directly from the Navigation Menu. The new entry can be placed anywhere in the existing hierarchy. By default, page name will be used as list entry name. The Map to an existing entry is used when you want the new page to highlight an existing, top level, menu entry. In the Icon option, you associate an icon with this list entry that will be displayed in the navigation menu.

CREATE REGION

After creating an application page, you add regions to it. A region is a fundamental building block used to organize and display content within a web page. It acts as a container for content, allowing developers to group related items together and manage them as a single unit.

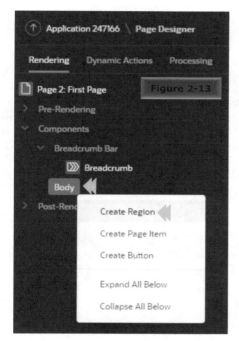

Figure 2-13

After creating the blank page, the page definitions will be displayed in page designer. Execute the following steps to create a region on this page.

1. Right-click the Body node, and select the first Create Region option from the context menu. A new region will be added under the Body node.

2. Using the Property Editor on the right side, set properties of the new region, as depicted in figure 2-14.

In the Title property, you provide a meaningful name to a region. At runtime, the title appears on top of the region.

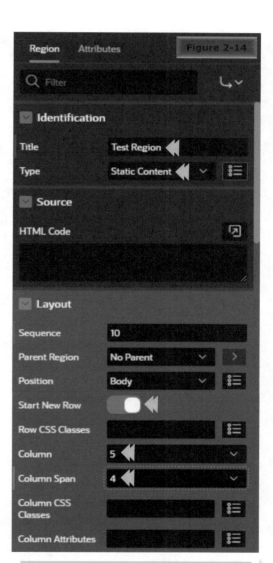

Figure 2-14

A Static Content Region is a type of region that allows developers to display static text or HTML content on a page. It is a simple and straightforward way to include non-changing information within an APEX application. Unlike other region types, static content regions do not interact with the database or perform any dynamic actions. Static Content Regions are particularly handy for adding informative elements to your application, enhancing user experience, and providing essential context to users as they interact with the application's dynamic components. This region will act as a container for page items that you will place on it in a moment.

The Layout section in the Property Editor serves the purpose of controlling the positioning and spacing of a selected component or region within a page. The Layout section allows developers to fine-tune the appearance and arrangement of the selected item. The Column property allows you to offset the region's position within the grid columns. For example, if you set the column value to 2, the region will be indented by two columns from the left. If the selected region is part of a grid layout, the Column Span property allows you to specify the number of columns the region should occupy. For example, in a 12-column grid layout, you can set the region to occupy 6 columns, taking up half of the available width. See next page for details.

NOTE
You can now test the page by clicking this Save and Run Page button available at top right in page designer.

A 12-columns grid layout is a commonly used grid system to organize and structure the page content. The 12-columns grid system allows you to distribute the content across the available columns, providing flexibility in designing the page layout.

In the Page Designer, you can easily resize and rearrange the components within the grid layout to achieve your desired design. Additionally, the grid layout will automatically adjust and adapt to different screen sizes, ensuring a responsive user experience across various devices. Using the 12-columns grid layout in APEX allows you to create visually appealing and user-friendly web pages while maintaining consistency and responsiveness.

ROW 1

REGION-1											
1	2	3	4	5	6	7	8	9	10	11	12

Start New Row = Turn ON
Column   = Automatic (i.e. 1)
Column Span = Automatic (i.e. 12)

ROW 2

REGION-2						REGION-3					
1	2	3	4	5	6	7	8	9	10	11	12

Start New Row = Turn ON
Column   = Automatic (i.e. 1)
Column Span   = 6 (i.e. 1 ➜ 6)

Start New Row = Turn OFF
Column   = 7
Column Span   = 6 (i.e. 7 ➜ 12)

ROW 3

REGION-4				REGION-5				REGION-6			
1	2	3	4	5	6	7	8	9	10	11	12

Start New Row = Turn ON
Column = Automatic (i.e. 1)
Column Span = 4 (i.e. 1 ➜ 4)

Start New Row = Turn OFF
Column = 5
Column Span = 4 (i.e. 5 ➜ 8)

Start New Row = Turn OFF
Column = 9
Column Span = 4 (i.e. 9 ➜ 12)

ROW 4

REGION-7								REGION-8			
1	2	3	4	5	6	7	8	9	10	11	12

Start New Row = Turn ON
Column   = Automatic (i.e. 1)
Column Span = 8 (i.e. 1 ➜ 8)

Start New Row = Turn OFF
Column = 9
Column Span = 4 (i.e. 9 ➜ 12)

The application pages created in Oracle APEX use a grid layout comprising 12 columns to position page elements. Eight regions are created on the adjacent page to explain how regions and other page components can be positioned on an application page using the 12 columns grid layout.

REGION-1

The first region is placed on row number 1 and it spans the complete gird, that is, it utilizes all the 12 columns. For this region, the Start New Row property is turned on to put the region on a new row. The Column property is set to Automatic which means that the region will not be indented and will start from column number 1. The default Automatic value for the Column Span property indicates that the region will occupy all 12 columns. With these three properties, Region-1 will span from column 1 to column 12.

REGION-2

The second region also starts on a new row just after the first region. Compare this value with the next region (Region-3), where it is turned off to place Region-3 to the right of Region-2 on the same row. This region starts from column number 1 and occupies 6 columns - i.e., from column 1 to column 6 to take up half of the available width.

REGION-3

The third region, as just mentioned, will be placed next to the second region. When you turn off the Start New Row property the page element is positioned next to the previous element. For this scenario, you have to set an appropriate value for the Column property. Here, we set it to 7 to start this region from column number 7. This region also spans 6 columns and takes up the remaining half of the grid layout.

REGION-4,5,6

As you can see, row number 3 has three regions, equally divided in the grid layout. Each region spans 4 columns and this is the value we set for the Column Span property for all the three regions. The first region spans from column number 1 to 4, the second one from 5 to 8, and the third one from 9 to 12.

REGION-7 and 8

The last two regions on row number 4 present a different combination in which Region-7 spans 8 columns - i.e., from column 1 to 8. Region-8 occupies the remaining 4 columns - i.e., from column 9 to 12. Looking at these examples, you have the flexibility to utilize various combinations of the three layout properties discussed here, and the given examples offer a clear insight into how you can effectively position and arrange elements on a single page.

CREATE LIST OF VALUES

Shared components are reusable elements that can be used across multiple pages and applications within an APEX workspace to maintain consistency and reduce duplication of code. Before creating page items, we will create some lists of values (LOV) shared components in this section. These shared components will be attached to some page items that you will create in the next section.

For creating Shared Components, you have to access its interface. There are a couple of options available on the application home page to access the Shared Components page. Here are the steps:

1. If you running the application, then click the Page 2 link in the developer toolbar. This action will take you to the page designer tab in your browser. Alternatively, if you are in the development mode, then you can click the App Builder menu to access the App Builder page. Here, you will see your application. Click the Edit icon to open the application home page.

Figure 2-15

2. On the application home page, you will see the two options to access the Shared Components page. Click on any of these two options. If you are in page designer, then you can access the Shared Components page using its icon available in the toolbar.

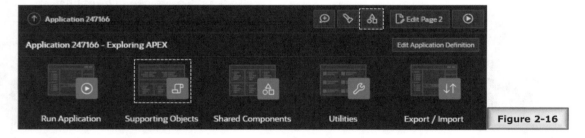

Figure 2-16

3. On the Shared Components page, select the Lists of Values option.

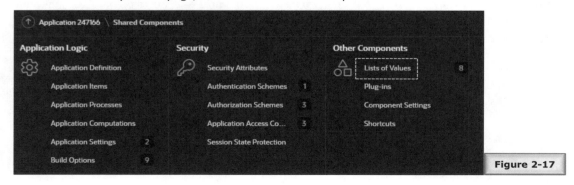

Figure 2-17

4. On the Lists of Values page click the Create button.

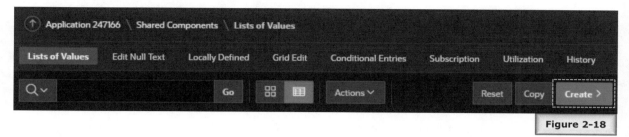

Figure 2-18

5. On the first wizard screen, select the From Scratch option to create a new list of values. Click Next to proceed to the next wizard screen.

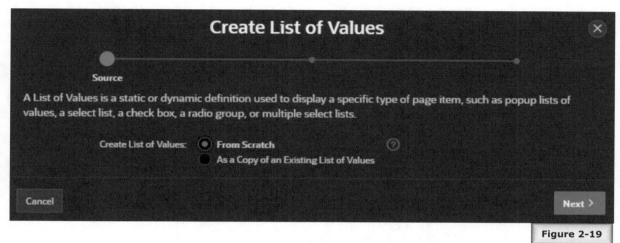

Figure 2-19

6. On the next wizard screen, enter Gender for the LOV name, and select the Static option for its Type. A Dynamic list of values defines a Data Source of either Local Database, REST Enabled SQL, or REST Data Source. On the other hand, a Static list of values is based on predefined display and return values. Click Next to proceed.

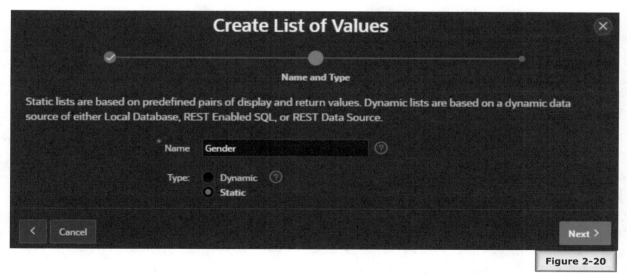

Figure 2-20

7. On the final wizard screen, enter display and return values as depicted in the following figure and click the Create List of Values button.

When creating an LOV, you typically define two important components: the Display Value and the Return Value. The purpose of having both Display Values and Return Values in LOVs is to provide a user-friendly interface for selecting values while ensuring that the underlying application logic can work appropriately with the selected value in the back-end.

For example, here you have an LOV for the "Gender" field with Display Values "Male," and "Female." When a user selects "Male" from the LOV, the item will display "Male" (Display Value) on the page. Simultaneously, the corresponding value, such as "Male" (Return Value), will be stored in the item's session state, which can be used for database operations or further processing in the application's business logic. You will experience this in the next chapter.

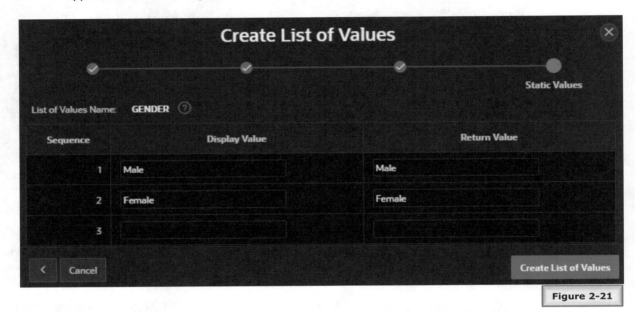

Figure 2-21

The new LOV named Gender will be listed on the Lists of Values page. The name of the LOV acts as a link. If you made any mistake while creating the LOV, then click this link. The LOVs definition will be opened in the Edit page, where you can modify it. If needed, you can also use the Edit page to add more entries to the LOV.

Figure 2-22

Using the same steps, create two more static LOVs (Section and Subjects) as illustrated in the following figures.

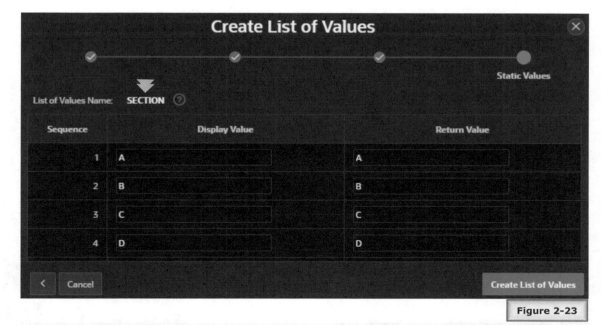

Figure 2-23

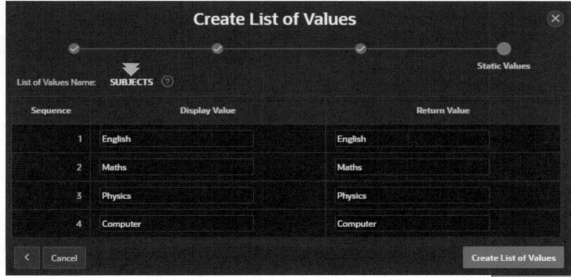

Figure 2-24

BUILD MEGA MENU

A menu refers to a user interface component that provides a hierarchical structure for organizing and navigating through various pages, reports, and other components within an application. Menus in APEX help users easily access different sections or functionalities of an application by providing a structured and intuitive navigation experience.

By default, the App Builder wizard creates a basic menu for the application comprising Home and Administration entries – see step 7 in the Create Application section earlier in this chapter. In this section, you will extend that default menu by adding some more entries.

1. Access the Shared Components page. Then, click the Navigation Menu entry in the Navigation and Search section. This will bring up the Lists page. On the Lists page, click the Navigation Menu entry. You will see the two default menu entries (Home and Administration) on the List Details page along with their respective target links. The pencil icon in the Edit column lets you modify the menu entries. Click the Create Entry button to add some top-level entries to the application menu.

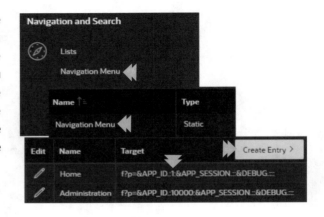

2. On the List Entry page, set properties for the new menu entry according to the adjacent table. The first attribute identifies the parent for this list entry. Since it is a top-level entry, we set the value to No Parent List Item. The Sequence determines the order of evaluation. The sequence of the Home entry is 10, so this entry will appear next to the Home entry. In the Image/Class property you specify an icon for the menu entry. The label of this entry is 'Setup,' and it has no target, meaning it is not associated with any application page. The entry you create in step 5 will appear under this 'Setup' menu entry as a sub-menu with a target page. Click the Create and Create Another button to save this entry and add another.

PROPERTY	VALUE
Parent List Entry	No Parent List Item
Sequence	20
Image/Class	fa-gear
List Entry Label	Setup
Target type	No Target

3. Set these properties for the new menu entry, which is also a top-level entry and it will appear next to the Setup menu.

PROPERTY	VALUE
Parent List Entry	No Parent List Item
Sequence	30
Image/Class	fa-table
List Entry Label	Transactions
Target type	No Target

4. Create this top-level entry for application reports.

PROPERTY	VALUE
Parent List Entry	No Parent List Item
Sequence	40
Image/Class	fa-print
List Entry Label	Reports
Target type	No Target

5. This one is a sub-menu entry and it will appear under the Setup menu – hence we set a value for the Parent List Entry property. The "Target Type" property refers to a setting that determines how a menu entry or link is associated with a specific target destination. This property is commonly used in various menu types to define where clicking on a menu item will navigate the user within the application. Here, we linked this menu entry to Page 3 that you will create in the next chapter. The last two properties are typically used in menus to visually indicate to users which menu entry corresponds to the currently displayed page. This menu entry will be highlighted when you call Page 3 and 4 at runtime as depicted in figure 2-25.

PROPERTY	VALUE
Parent List Entry	Setup
Sequence	100
Image/Class	fa-address-card-o
List Entry Label	Students Profile
Target type	Page in this Application
Page	3
List Entry Current for Pages Type	Comma Delimited Page List
List Entry Current for Condition	3,4

This is the final output of the application mega menu that you will see at runtime. The Students Profile menu appears as a sub-menu under the Setup menu.

Figure 2-25

A page item refers to a user interface component that allows users to interact with the application. These page items are used to capture input from users, display information, and hold values that can be used in various parts of the application.

In this section, you will create some commonly used page items, such as Text Field, Radio Group, Switch, Select List, Number Field, Date Picker, and Check Boxes. Each page item has a unique name and can be associated with a database column, or a session state. Page items are used to capture user input, which can then be used in SQL queries, PL/SQL processes, or validations to manipulate data or perform various actions within the application. Developers can control the behavior and appearance of page items through various attributes and settings, such as names, default values, and display conditions. Execute the following steps to add some page items to the Test Region created in Page 2.

1. Click the application ID breadcrumb link (Application 250373) to access the application home page. Note that your application ID will be different from the one shown here.

2. On the application home page, click page 2 (2 - First Page) to open the page in page designer.

3. Right-click the Test Region, and select Create Page Item from the context menu. This will add a new page item named P2_NEW under the Test Region.

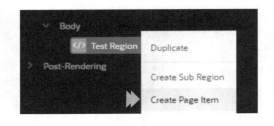

4. In the Property Editor to your right, set Name, Type, and Label for the page item. Item names are prefixed with the letter P, which stands for Page, followed by the page number. Here, the prefix P2 denotes that this page item belongs to page 2. The Text Field type is a basic input field where users can enter text or numeric values. Labels are essential for improving the user interface and guiding users to understand the purpose or expected input for different elements in the application. Click the Save and Run Page button and observe how the page item appears in the Test Region.

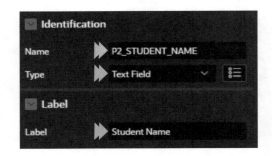

5. Again, right-click the Test Region, and select Create Page Item from the context menu. Set the three properties for this item as well. It is a date type item that opens a date picker as a popup and allows users to pick a date. Save and run the page to see this item on the page. When you click the Select Date icon, a mini calendar appears from where you can pick a date to set students date of birth.

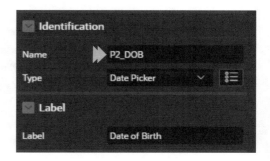

6. Create another page item to record the student's gender. It's a Radio Group type item and it will display the Values Male and Female using the Gender Shared Component. The Radio Group item type is a group of options represented as radio buttons, allowing users to select a single option. Set the highlighted values for this page item and then save and run the page to see how it appears on the page. In the Number of Columns property, you enter the number of radio group columns to display. For example, a value of 2 would display two columns, so if there were five values then it would display over three rows. The Type property in the List of Values section contains four values - Shared Component, SQL Query, Static Values, and Function Body returning SQL Query. The Shared Components is a list of values that is based on a predefined list of values, defined in Shared Components - for example, Gender. The Dynamic list of values is based on the SQL Query you enter. The Static list of values is based on the text value you enter. And the final option returns a dynamic list of values based on the SQL Query returned by the Function you enter.

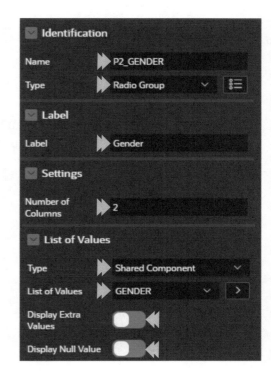

7. This one is a Number Field item and it receives numeric values. This item type automatically validates that the value is a number. Here, you will enter student's class.

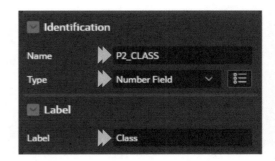

8. Add a new page item under the previous one and set properties according to the adjacent screenshot. It is a Select List, which is based on the Section LOV. a Select List is a type of item that allows users to choose an option from a list of predefined values. Select lists are commonly used in forms to provide users with a set of choices to select from. Here, you will select student's section i.e., A, B, C, or D.

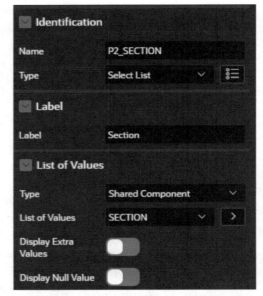

9. The Disability page item is a Switch type item. A Switch item is a special type of page item that allows users to make binary choices, typically represented as a toggle switch (e.g., on/off or yes/no).

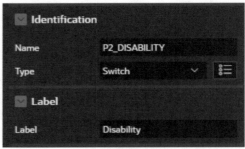

10. This marks the final page item belonging to the Checkbox Group type, showcasing the preferred subjects of the students. A Checkbox Group is a type of page item that allows users to select multiple options from a list of predefined values. It is presented as a group of checkboxes, where each checkbox represents a distinct option.

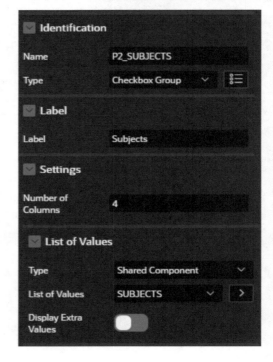

11. Now add a button to the region. Right-click the Test Region and select Create Button from the context menu. A button will be added just under the last page item. Set properties of this button as illustrated in the screenshot. The button name is SAVE and this value is used to reference the button when it is clicked. When this page is submitted, the value of REQUEST is set to this button name. The Region property is set to Test Region to display the button in this region. When you select the Copy position, the button is placed on the right side of the region at runtime. The Text with Icon value displays the label 'Save' and an icon on the button. You can select an icon for the button using the adjacent list of values icon. By turning on the Hot property, the button is displayed in a dark color. In the Action property, you select the action to be performed when this button is clicked. By default, the value of this property is set to Submit Page that submits the current page with a REQUEST value equal to the Button Name. We'll dig deeper in the next chapter to understand the whole process.

Save and run the page. The region and the page items should look similar to this screenshot. Here, we used some LOVs to ensure data integrity. LOVs are a mechanism to provide a list of selectable values for a field, typically in the context of item selection, filtering, or validation. The main benefit of using LOVs in Oracle APEX is to enhance the user experience and improve data integrity by ensuring that users choose valid and consistent values. Click the Save button. Clicking the Save button will trigger the submission of the page. However, no action will take place, and the student's record will not be saved anywhere. The reason is that there is currently no backend database table to store the student's information. In the upcoming chapter, we will address this by creating a database table and utilizing Oracle APEX's built-in Form feature to save the student's records.

WHAT YOU LEARNED

▶ Crafted the fundamental structure of you first application in Oracle APEX.

　　▶ Learned how to perform different operations on the application using the application home page features.

　　　▶ Created your first application page.

　　　▶ Created a region on the page and went through 12-columns grid layout to position page elements.

　　▶ Created LOV Shared Components.

▶ Created page items and associated LOVs to ensure data integrity.

INTERACTIVE REPORT

& FORM

3

INTERACTIVE REPORT

An interactive report is a powerful data grid component that allows users to interactively view data in a tabular format. It provides a rich set of features such as sorting, filtering, highlighting, and dynamic actions, enabling users to explore and analyze data in a flexible and user-friendly manner.

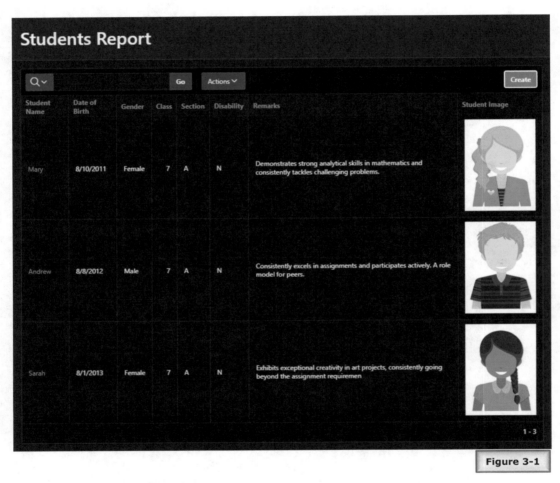

Figure 3-1

Creating an interactive report involves defining the SQL query or selecting a table/view as the data source. You can then customize the columns, sorting options, filtering criteria, and other attributes of the report.

Interactive reports are particularly useful when you want to provide users with an intuitive and flexible way to explore and work with large datasets. They eliminate the need for users to write custom queries or rely on static reports, as they can interactively control how the data is presented and manipulated within the application.

Overall, interactive reports in Oracle APEX enhance the user experience, improve data analysis capabilities, and allow users to gain valuable insights from their data without requiring extensive technical knowledge or coding skills.

Key features of an interactive report in Oracle APEX include:

Sorting

Users can click on column headers to sort the data in ascending or descending order based on that column's values.

Filtering

Users can apply filters to the data, allowing them to narrow down the results to specific criteria.

Pagination

The report can be divided into pages, displaying a limited number of rows per page, and users can navigate through the pages.

Searching

Users can search for specific values within the report, making it easier to find relevant information.

Highlighting

Users can highlight specific rows or cells based on conditions, making it visually easy to identify important data.

Exporting

Users can export the data in various formats, such as CSV, Excel, or PDF.

Dynamic Actions

Interactive reports support dynamic actions, enabling you to create custom interactions based on user actions (e.g., automatically refresh the interactive report every time the user types something in the "Search" field).

Chart View

The Chart View in an interactive report allows you to represent data from your report in graphical formats like bar charts, line charts, pie charts, and more. It is an excellent way to visualize the data and gain insights quickly.

Pivot View

The Pivot View in an interactive report allows you to pivot your data, effectively changing the way it is presented in the report. Instead of displaying the data in rows and columns, you can transpose rows to columns and vice versa, which can be useful for different data analysis scenarios.

Group By View

The Group By View in an interactive report allows you to group the data based on one or more columns. It creates a summary view of your data with grouped data and the corresponding aggregates. This is useful when you want to see data summarized and categorized based on specific criteria.

FORM

A form in Oracle APEX allows you to perform Create, Read, Update, and Delete (CRUD) operations on your data. Form pages are essential components in creating data-driven applications with Oracle APEX. They provide an efficient and user-friendly way for users to interact with the data stored in the database.

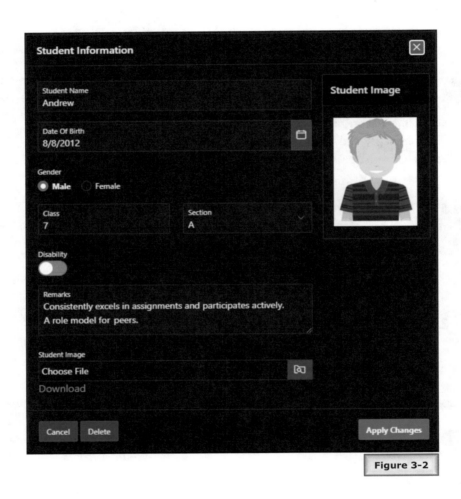

Figure 3-2

In Oracle Application Express (APEX), a form page is a type of page that allows users to interactively create, read, update, and delete (CRUD) data in a database table or view. It provides a user-friendly interface for managing data records, and it's one of the most common components used in web applications to handle data manipulation.

When you create a form page in Oracle APEX, it generates a set of input elements such as text fields, date pickers, select lists, and buttons that correspond to the columns in the underlying table or view. Users can then enter data into these input elements to add or edit records in the database.

Here are some key features of a form page in Oracle APEX:

Data Input

Users can enter data into the form fields to add or update records in the database. In Oracle APEX, data entry and data modification are common tasks performed using forms. A form in APEX allows users to interactively enter new data, update existing data, and delete records in the database. APEX provides declarative options to create forms based on tables, views, or custom SQL queries, making it easy to build data entry and modification interfaces without writing code. By using APEX forms, you can quickly build data entry and modification interfaces with minimal effort, allowing users to interact with the database efficiently and securely. The declarative nature of APEX forms reduces the need for custom coding and accelerates application development.

Data Validation

You can define validation rules on the form elements to ensure data integrity and correctness before it is submitted to the database. Data validation in Oracle APEX forms is vital for ensuring data integrity and user-friendly interactions. APEX offers two main types of validations: client-side and server-side. Client-side validations take place in the user's browser before data submission, providing immediate feedback and reducing server round-trips. Built-in validation types include checks for required fields, format, and length, while custom JavaScript allows for more complex validations. On the other hand, server-side validations occur on the server after form submission, ensuring business rules and data integrity are upheld securely. Server-side validations are especially important for enforcing unique key constraints and applying intricate business logic. By combining both types of validations, APEX applications can maintain data accuracy, enhance the user experience, and safeguard against manipulation or data inconsistencies.

DML Operations

Oracle APEX handles the data manipulation language (DML) operations (insert, update, and delete) automatically, so you don't need to write SQL code for basic CRUD operations. The Automatic Row Processing (DML) feature significantly accelerates application development in Oracle APEX, making it easier to create data-driven applications that interact with the database seamlessly.

Dynamic Actions

You can define dynamic actions on form items to perform specific actions based on user interactions. Dynamic actions are a declarative way to specify specific actions that should occur based on user interactions with form items. These actions can include showing or hiding items, setting item values, executing JavaScript, refreshing regions, and more. When creating a dynamic action, developers define the event that triggers it, the item or component it applies to, and any optional conditions for execution. Dynamic actions allow developers to create interactive and responsive forms without writing custom JavaScript code. Examples include updating total amounts when quantity or price fields change, showing dependent select lists, and submitting forms on pressing the "Enter" key in a specific item.

Processing

APEX handles form submission, data processing, and error handling, providing a smooth user experience. In Oracle APEX, form submission, data processing, and error handling are seamlessly managed through a well-structured flow. When a user submits a form, APEX automatically captures the input data and processes it using declarative DML processes. These processes handle data insertion, updating, and deletion based on the form inputs. If the data meets validation criteria, APEX saves it to the database. However, if any errors occur during the process, APEX provides built-in error handling mechanisms. It displays error messages to the user, highlighting the specific invalid fields and explaining the corrective actions required. Developers can customize error messages, define conditional validations, and set up error handling actions to ensure a smooth user experience. APEX also offers options for transaction processing and rollbacks in case of critical errors, guaranteeing data integrity and consistent form submissions.

Conditions

You can apply conditional rendering to show or hide form elements based on certain conditions. These conditions are based on item values, application variables, session state, or expressions. When a page is rendered, APEX evaluates these conditions and dynamically renders or hides the form elements accordingly. For instance, you can show additional fields based on a checkbox selection, enable a field only if a certain condition is met, or make certain fields mandatory under specific circumstances.

OBJECT BROWSER

The Object Browser is an Oracle APEX feature that allows users to explore and interact with various database objects, such as tables, views, sequences, triggers, and procedures, within a schema. It provides a visual interface for browsing the schema objects that are accessible to the current database user.

The Object Browser provides a convenient way for users to create and interact with the database objects and perform database-related tasks without the need for direct SQL commands. It is a valuable tool for database administrators and developers working on database-centric applications within the APEX environment.

Prior to creating the interactive report and form pages, execute the following steps to create a database table interactively through the Object Browser. This table will be used in the interactive report and form to view and store students' information.

1. From the main SQL Workshop menu, select the first Object Browser option. This action will bring up the Object Browser page.

2. In the left pane, click the Create Database Objects drop-down list, and select the Table option to create a new table. A new page labeled 'Create Table' will pop up to receive the definitions of the new table.

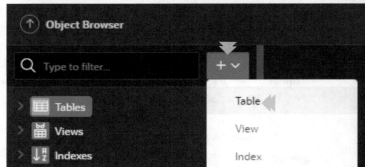

52

Fill in the Create Table form as illustrated in the following figure. Use the Edit and Add Column buttons to fill in the columns' details. After completing the table definitions, click the Create Table button.

A In the Table Name you provide a descriptive name for the new table. The name must conform to Oracle naming conventions and cannot contain spaces, or start with a number or underscore.

B Then, you click the Edit button to enable the first default row in the Columns section. Use the Add Column button to add more rows.

C First, you enter a name for the column – for example, STUDENT_ID. Then, you select a Data Type for the column from the drop-down list. Here, the STUDENT_ID column is a numeric column, so we selected the NUMBER data type. We also marked this column as Not Null and Primary Key to store unique IDs for each student.

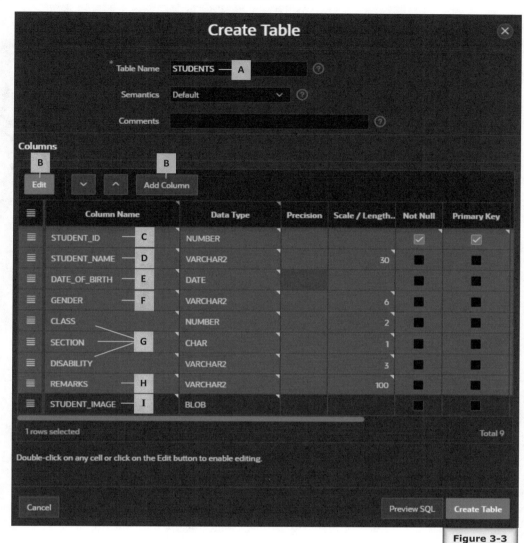

Figure 3-3

D The data type of the STUDENT_NAME column is VARCHAR2(30). This data type is used to store variable-length character strings, and in this case, you can store a name up to 30 characters.

E The data type of the DATE_OF_BIRTH column is DATE. The value in this column will be stored in mm/dd/yyyy format. Therefore, the length of this data type is fixed and handled automatically by the database.

F The GENDER column will store either 'Male' or 'Female'. Therefore, its length is set to 6 characters to accommodate both values.

G The CLASS column will store values from 1 to 10. The SECTION column will store values from A to D, which you created as LOVs in the previous chapter. The DISABILITY column will store either 'Yes' or 'No,' also created as an LOV in the previous chapter.

H In the REMARKS column you can input any type of details about the student. The length of this column is 100 characters.

I The final STUDENT_IMAGE column is a BLOB (Binary Large Object) type column, which is typically used to store binary data, such as images, audio, video, and document files. Here, it will store the images of students. Click the Create Table button.

After clicking the Create Table button, you will be taken back to the Object Browser page displaying the new STUDENTS table on the left side under the Tables node, and its column definitions on the right side. As illustrated in the figure below, there are several tabs that reveal different information for this table. Here are some briefs about these tabs:

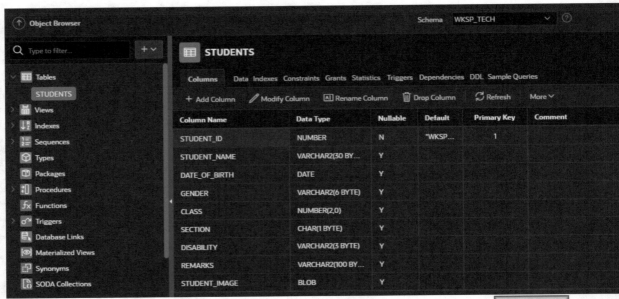

Figure 3-4

Columns

The Columns tab in the Object Browser provides information about the structure and attributes of database objects, such as tables. When you select a specific object from the list, the Columns tab displays the following details for each column within that object:

- Column Name: The name of the column in the database object.

- Data Type: The data type of the data stored in the column (e.g., VARCHAR2, NUMBER, DATE). For numeric data types, you can specify precision, which indicates the total number of digits allowed, and scale, which indicates the number of decimal places allowed. For example, consider the CLASS column, which has a precision of 2 and a scale of 0 (meaning no decimal places allowed).

- Nullable: Specifies whether the column allows NULL values or not. The 'N' in the STUDENT_ID column indicates that this column must have some value – all the remaining columns can be null.

- Default: If defined, it shows the default value for the column.

- Primary Key: Indicates whether the column is part of the primary key. In a database table, a primary key is a special column or set of columns that uniquely identifies each row in the table. It serves as a unique identifier for each record and ensures that there are no duplicate rows in the table. The STUDENT_ID column in this table is identified as the primary key, and it serves the purpose of preventing duplicate values. Note that the value for this column will be generated automatically. If you look at the CREATE TABLE statement under the DDL tab, you will see "GENERATED BY DEFAULT ON NULL AS IDENTITY" clause using which Oracle generates a value for the identity column (STUDENT_ID) if you provide a NULL value or no value at all.

- Comments: Any additional comments or descriptions related to the column.

- Add Column: The Add Column option under the Columns tab in the Object Browser allows users to add a new column to an existing database table. This option is particularly useful when you need to extend the structure of an existing table by introducing additional attributes (columns) to accommodate new data requirements.

- Modify Column: The Modify Column option under the Columns tab in the Object Browser allows users to alter the properties of an existing column in a database table. This option is used when you need to change the data type, nullability, default value, or other attributes of an existing column without recreating the entire table.

- Rename Column: The Rename Column option under the Columns tab in the Object Browser allows users to change the name of an existing column in a database table. This option is useful when you want to give the column a more descriptive or appropriate name or when you need to update the column name due to changes in business requirements.

- Drop Column: The Drop Column option under the Columns tab in the Object Browser allows users to remove an existing column from a database table. This option is useful when you no longer need a specific column in the table or when you want to restructure the table by eliminating unnecessary attributes.

Figure 3-5

Data

The Data tab in the Object Browser allows you to view the actual data present in the selected database object. When you choose an object (e.g., a table) from the list and switch to the Data tab, you can browse through the rows and columns of the table and see the data stored in it. This tab presents a paginated grid-like view of the data, enabling you to navigate through multiple records. The Data tab has the following options:

- Insert Row: The Insert Row option enables you to add new records (rows) to the table. It provides a user-friendly interface for entering data directly into the table.

- Columns: Using the Columns option, you can select the columns to display in the lower data pane.

- Filter: The Filter option enables you to apply specific conditions or filters to the displayed data. You can use this option to narrow down the results and view specific subsets of data that meet your criteria.

- Load Data: Load Data refers to the functionality that allows users to import data from external sources into a database table. It provides a convenient way to bulk load data into a table without manually entering each record one by one. Supported formats are csv, xlsx, txt, xml, and json.

- Download: By clicking the Download option, you get the data in Microsoft Excel format.

Execute the following steps to create the Interactive Report and Form pages interactively to view and store students' information.

1. On the application home page, click the Create Page button and then select the Interactive Report option on the first wizard screen.

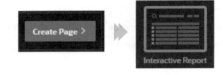

2. On the next wizard screen, fill in the Page Definition section as illustrated here. In the initial Page Number and Name attributes, you provide a unique number and a name for the interactive report, and mark it as a 'Normal' page. The Normal page covers the entire screen. Enabling the Include Form Page flag creates a form page along with the report page. Using the Form page, you can perform DML operations on the specified database table. In this context, the form page is numbered 4 and labeled as 'Student Information,' which will appear at the top of the interactive report page during runtime. We marked the Form page as a Modal Dialog. A modal dialog is a window overlay placed within the visible area of the screen, persistently active and focused until the user dismisses (closes) it. While the dialog is open, the underlying page is obscured by a grayed-out background, restricting the user's interaction with the rest of the page.

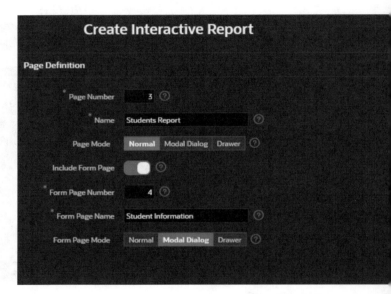

3. In the Data Source section, select the Local Database option for the Data Source because we will be interacting with the STUDENTS table locally. Using the icon appearing next to the Table/View Name property, select the STUDENTS table. The local database option allows you to connect directly to a database schema within the same Oracle database instance where your APEX application resides. The REST Enabled SQL Service in Oracle APEX allows you to connect to a remote database using a RESTful service. This service acts as an intermediary layer between your APEX application and the remote database. The REST Data Source option in Oracle APEX allows you to connect to external RESTful APIs and retrieve data from them. With this option, you can configure APEX to make

HTTP requests to external RESTful services, retrieve JSON or XML responses, and then process and display the retrieved data within your APEX application. This is helpful when you need to integrate data from various sources or leverage third-party APIs to enhance the functionality of your APEX application.

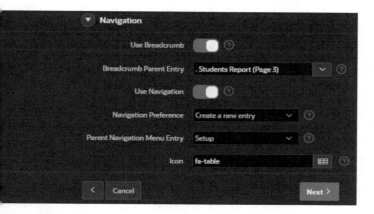

4. The navigation section refers to the settings related to how users can navigate to and access the page within your application. When creating a page in Oracle APEX, you can specify whether you want to create a breadcrumb entry for this page. The Navigation option is used while creating a page to specify how the page will be navigated to and accessed within the application. Here, the page name will be used as menu entry name and it will appear under the Setup entry. You can use the icon picker to pick a different icon for this entry. Click Next to proceed.

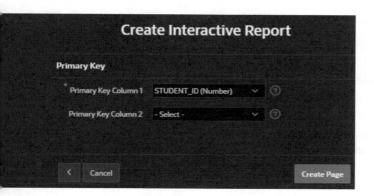

5. On the final wizard screen, select the STUDENT_ID primary key column. Specifying a primary key column while creating a page in Oracle APEX is essential for data integrity and proper functioning of the application. A primary key is a unique identifier for each record in a table, and it serves several crucial purposes, such as maintaining data integrity, enabling data relationships, improving data retrieval performance, and ensuring proper data modification and referential integrity within the application's database. Click the Create Page button to complete the page creation process.

After creating the pages, you will be landed on the Page Designer interface showing the definitions of the interactive report page – Page 3. When you create an Interactive Report page using the Page Creation Wizard in Oracle APEX, the following interactive report components are typically created:

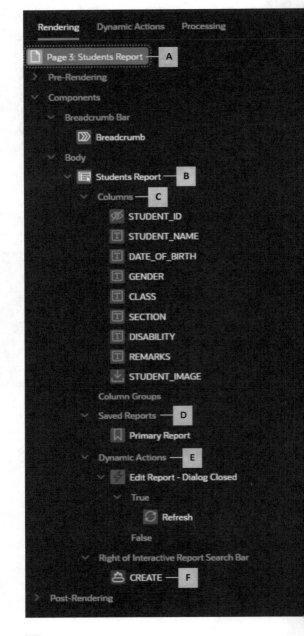

A The Root Node: When you click the root node under the Rendering tab, you see the main properties of the interactive report page in the Properties editor on the right side. For example, you see the Page Name, Title, and Page Mode properties you set while creating the page. If needed, you can modify these properties.

B Interactive Report Region: The Students Report is the main region that displays the interactive report. It shows various attributes related to the interactive report's appearance, behavior, and data source set up through the wizard. The Source section of this region reveals from where the data in this interactive report will be displayed. It contains the auto-generated SQL query in the Source section of the property editor that fetches data from the STUDENTS table.

C Report Columns: Each column from the table is added to the report. These columns display data from the underlying data source and provide options for sorting, filtering, and formatting. The STUDENT_ID column is marked as a hidden column by the page creation wizard. It is a primary key in the STUDENTS table and does not display in the interactive report at runtime, but it is referenceable.

D Saved Reports: Besides the Primary Report (the default), you can create different variations of an interactive report including Alternative, Private, and Public. The primary report is the main default report that is created and configured to display data from the data source. An Alternative report is a separate report that can be switched with the primary report dynamically and it allows you to display different views of the same data or provide alternative ways of presenting information. Alternative reports can be useful for offering users different perspectives on the data without creating entirely new pages. A Private report is a report that a specific user or developer creates and customizes for their personal use. It is not visible or accessible to other users of the application. Private reports are often used for ad-hoc analysis or experimentation without affecting the main reports available to all users. A Public report is a report that is made available to all users of the application. It is typically designed and configured by developers or administrators to provide consistent data analysis capabilities to all users. Public reports are visible and accessible to all authorized users of the application. You will see some of these variations in action in a subsequent chapter.

E Dynamic Actions: The default Dialog Closed Dynamic Action refreshes the interactive report when you close the form page. This refresh ensures the display of new data or any modifications you made to existing data.

F Create Button: This auto-generated button is used to call the form page for adding a new record. This behavior is set in the Target property of this button. Clicking the Page 4 button in the Target property opens the Link Builder dialog box, where the form page (4) is set as the target for the Create button. See further details in the 'Create Link' section ahead.

Enter 4 in the page navigation option in the toolbar to open the form page (Page 4) in page designer. Here are some details of this page.

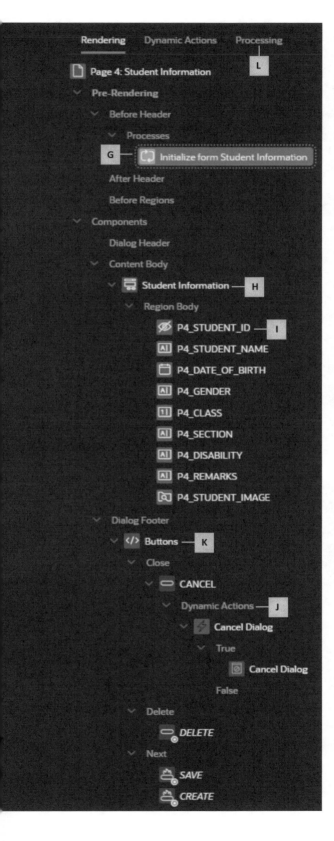

G Initialize Form Process: When a form page is requested by a user or when the user navigates to the page, Oracle APEX goes through the form initialization process to set up the necessary components and data for the page.

H Student Information: It is a Form type region. The data from the STUDENTS table columns is fetched into the page items created under this region – see the Source section of this region in the property editor.

I Page Items: The wizard creates the same number and types of page items as those present in the base table. For instance, the page item P4_STUDENT_NAME is a text field that displays data from VARCHAR2 type columns. Similarly, the page item P4_DATE_OF_BIRTH is a Date Picker used for Date type columns. The P4_STUDENT_IMAGE type is set to File Browse, which displays a text field along with a Browse... button. This button allows users to locate and upload a file from their local file system. When looking at the Source of all these page items, you'll notice that they are all mapped to their corresponding columns in the STUDENTS table.

J Dynamic Actions: The Cancel Dialog dynamic action is associated with the CANCEL button and it closes the form page when the Cancel button is clicked. The dynamic action is defined under the Dynamic Actions tab. Since it is associated with the CANCEL button, it appears as a reference under the button.

K Buttons: In addition to the CANCEL button, the wizard creates three more buttons (DELETE, SAVE, and CREATE) to handle DML operations on the STUDENTS table through the form. When you click the DELETE button, an SQL delete action is submitted to the page's Automatic Row Processing (DML) process (discussed next) to delete the record being displayed in the form. The SAVE button triggers an update action, while the CREATE button triggers an INSERT action. See the Behavior section of these buttons in the property editor.

L Processing: When you click the Processing tab, you see a process of Form - Automatic Row Processing (DML) type. It is a predefined process type that simplifies the process of performing Data Manipulation Language (DML) operations, such as Insert, Update, and Delete, on database records using a form page. This process automates the handling of database interactions when users submit a form using the DELETE, SAVE, and CREATE buttons. The other process 'Close Dialog' closes the form page when CREATE, SAVE, or DELETE buttons are clicked. See the Server-side Condition section of this process in the property editor.

Execute the following steps to associate some form page items with the LOVs you created in the previous chapter.

1. On the form page (Page 4), click the P4_GENDER item and set the adjacent properties. In the first property, we changed the type of this page item from Text Field to Radio Group to display the two values from the Gender LOV. The remaining properties were explained in the previous chapter. We set 'Male' as the default value for this item. A default value for a page item allows you to prepopulate the item with a specific value when the page is initially loaded or accessed. This can be helpful for providing users with a starting value.

PROPERTY	VALUE
Type	Radio Group
Number of Columns	2
Type (List of Values)	Shared Component
List of Values	GENDER
Display Extra Values	Turn Off
Display Null Value	Turn Off
Type (Default)	Static
Static Value	Male

2. Click the P4_SECTION item and set the adjacent properties.

PROPERTY	VALUE
Type	Select List
Type (List of Values)	Shared Component
List of Values	SECTION
Display Extra Values	Turn Off
Display Null Value	Turn Off

3. Click the P4_DISABILITY item and set the adjacent properties.

PROPERTY	VALUE
Type	Switch

4. Click the P4_REMARKS item and set it type to Textarea. A Textarea page item is a user interface element used to capture and display multi-line text input from users. It provides a larger input area compared to a standard text field, allowing users to enter or view more extensive text content, such as comments, descriptions, or notes. The Height property of a Textarea page item refers to the vertical size or dimension of the Textarea input field on a page. This property allows you to specify how many rows of text should be visible in the Textarea when the page is rendered. Users can then enter and edit text within the visible area of the Textarea, and if the content exceeds the visible area, a scrollbar may appear to allow scrolling through the content. The last two properties make this item mandatory. The required template places a red triangle at top left to visually indicate this item as mandatory.

PROPERTY	VALUE
Type	Textarea
Height (Appearance)	2
Template	Required - Floating
Value Required	Turn On

INSERT DATA

We now have a form to insert data into the STUDENTS table. Forms are designed with input fields that correspond to table columns. Users enter data in the form fields, and upon submission, APEX processes the data, validates it, and inserts it into the table.

Execute the following steps to insert some data into the STUDENTS table using the form page and then view the data on the interactive report page.

1. In Page Designer, switch back to the interactive report page – Page 3. Click the Save and Run page button. The interactive report page is displayed, currently showing no data as there are no student records available. The interactive report page can also be accessed by clicking the Students Profile option in the main application menu.

2. Click the Create button on the interactive report page to access the form page. Fill in the form page as shown in here to create Andew's record. Pick a date for Date of Birth by clicking the calendar icon being displayed in this page item. Use the Browse button to upload his image, which is available in Chapter 3 folder in the book's source code. Click the Create button on the form page to save this record. You will be taken back to the interactive report page by the Close Dialog process specified under the Processing tab on the form page. The Refresh Dynamic Action specified in the interactive report will update the report to show Andrew's record.

Using the Edit icon in the first interactive report column, you can modify this record. When you click this icon, the form page re-appears with Andrew's record and you can make modifications to any field. The form also allows you to delete this record using the Delete button. If you look at the Confirmation section of the Delete button in the property editor, you will see this message &APP_TEXT$DELETE_MSG!RAW. It is a substitution string representing an application or system text message that confirms the deletion. To override this message with your own text, go to Application > Shared Components > Text Messages and create a message named DELETE_MSG.

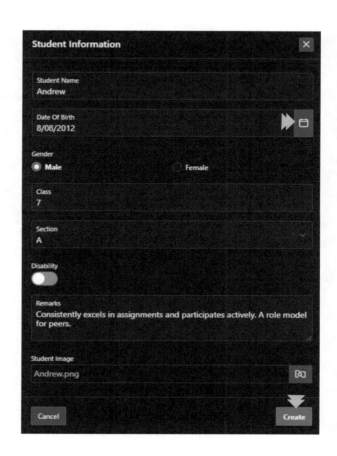

The first student record appears on the interactive report. The Edit icon provided in the first report column allows you to modify a record. Let's tweak some attributes of this report to learn some more development techniques.

In this task, your objective is to transform students' names into clickable links that will open the form page for modifying student records. Additionally, you will replace the 'Download' link currently displayed in the 'Student Image' column with the actual images of the students.

1. Click the Page 3 link in the developer toolbar to open the interactive report page in page designer.

2. Expand the Columns node under the Students Report region, and click the STUDENT_NAME column to select this column. In the property editor, change the Type of this column from Plain Text to Link. Then, scroll down to the Link section in the property editor. Click the No Link Defined button in front of the Target property. Set the link attributes in the Link Builder dialog box as illustrated here.

   The Link Builder dialog box is a user interface component that allows developers to create and configure hyperlinks or links between different pages within an application or external URLs. Here, we are creating a link to access the form page (Page 4) from the interactive report page.

   In the Name section of the Link Builder, you specify the name of the page item on the target page that you want to set a value for. This is the page item that will receive the value passed from the source page. Here, we are setting value for P4_STUDENT_ID, which is an item on page 4.

   Then, you provide a Value that you want to assign to the specified page item on the target page. Here the value is the id of the selected student derived from the STUDENT_ID column in the interactive report. Note that column names are enclosed in # symbol when you specify them as value. You can select both Name and Value from the adjacent LOVs. The Clear Cache attribute resets the form page (Page 4) to display information of the selected student.

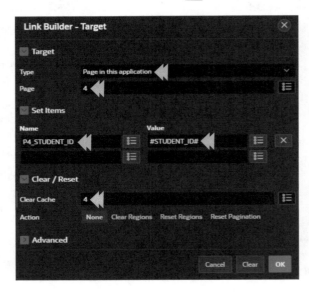

In the current scenario, the interactive report displays a list of students, and you want to allow users to click on a student's name to navigate to the form page where they can edit the student's details. You set the student's ID as a value for the page item (P4_STUDENT_ID) on the target form page. This way, when the user arrives at the form page, the student's ID is already set, and the form can use that ID to pre-populate the items on the form page with the correct student's information.

3. Click the OK button to close the Link Builder dialog box. Click the Save and Run Page button. The student's name should now be displayed as a link. Click the name to see Andrew's details on the form page. Modify some values on the form page and click the Apply Changes button. When you click the Apply Changes button, the default DML process defined under the Processing tab on Page 4 commits all modifications to the STUDENTS table. Observe that the modifications are reflected immediately on the interactive report.

4. The interactive report now features two edit links to access the form page. Let's remove the default edit link. Click the Students Report interactive report region on Page 3. In the property editor, click the Attributes tab. Select the value Exclude Link Column for the Link Column property. Save and run the page. The default edit link will be taken away from the interactive report and you can access the form page using the students' names.

5. To view the uploaded student images, access Page 3 in the page designer and click on the STUDENT_IMAGE column. Change the Type property of this column from Download BLOB to Display Image. Save your changes and run the page. Andrew's image should now appear in the last column of the report.

The search bar in an interactive report provides users with a convenient and powerful way to search and filter data directly within the report. It enables users to quickly locate specific information without having to scroll through large datasets manually.

Clicking a column heading (for example, Student Name) renders a small menu. The menu allows you to filter, sort, hide, and apply control breaks on the interactive report data.

The Actions Menu empowers you with tools to manipulate and analyze data in interactive reports. It offers options for filtering, sorting, grouping, and highlighting data, as well as creating charts and computed columns. Users can export data in various formats, print reports, and customize column visibility. The menu enhances data exploration, visualization, and customization within Oracle APEX applications. We'll explore the Actions Menu in the next chapter.

ALIGN PAGE ITEMS

The page creation wizard aligns form page items vertically, with each item stacked on top of the other. This vertical alignment makes it easier for users to navigate and interact with the form, especially when entering data from top to bottom. However, you can customize the layout and alignment of page items to better suit your specific design preferences and user interface requirements.

Execute the following instruction to align the Section item with the Class item on the form page.

Open the form page Page 4 in page designer. Click the P4_SECTION page item, and turn off the Start New Row property. By turning off this property, the P4_SECTION will be placed next to the previous page item i.e., P4_CLASS. This change is also reflected under the Layout tab in the central pane of page designer. For further details, see 12-Columns Grid Layout in the previous chapter. You can test this alignment by saving and running the page. Note that a modal Oracle APEX page cannot be run directly. In Oracle APEX, modal pages are designed to be displayed within a modal dialog framework, which is typically triggered by an action on another page. Modal dialogs provide a way to present additional information or allow users to perform specific tasks without navigating away from the current page. Since the form modal page cannot be run or accessed directly like a normal page, you have to run the interactive report page first and then click the student's name to see the form page.

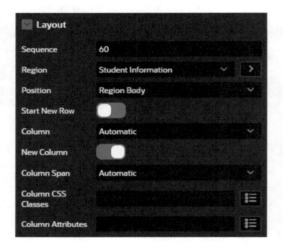

In a previous section, you learned how to display images in interactive reports. In this section, you will display the same image on the form page. When you navigate to the form page and retrieve a record, the image associated with that record will be displayed in an image item.

1. In page designer, right-click the Content Body node and select Create Region from the context menu. This action will add a new Static Content region under the Student Information form region. Set properties of the new region as shown in the adjacent table. The region will act as a container for the student's image. It will appear next to the Student Information region and will span 3 columns. The Standard template puts a border around the region with the title appearing on top.

PROPERTY	VALUE
Title	Student Image
Start New Row	Turn off
Column Span	3
Template	Standard

2. Right-click the Student Image region, and select Create Page Item from the context menu. Set properties of the new page item as shown in the adjacent table. The item will display the image. In the Source section, you specify the source of the image. Save the page and then access it from the interactive report page. The form page should resemble figure 3-2 illustrated at the beginning of this chapter.

PROPERTY	VALUE
Name	P4_IMAGE
Type	Display Image
Label	*Delete the label*
Form Region (Source)	Student Information
Column	STUDENT_IMAGE
Data Type	BLOB

3. Create two more student records using the information provided in Figure 3-1.

WHAT YOU LEARNED

▶ Created Interactive Report and Form pages with all basic functionalities without writing any code.

  ▶ Learned about the key features of Interactive Report and Form.

    ▶ Learned about Object Browser and created a table interactively.

      ▶ Went through regions, page items, buttons, dynamic actions, and processes.

        ▶ Utilized the LOVs created in the previous chapter.

      ▶ Learned the execution process of insert, update, and delete DML operations.

    ▶ Learned how to create links to associate two application pages.

  ▶ Learned how to display images in Interactive Report and Form.

▶ Learned how page items are aligned side-by-side.

4

MASTER DETAIL & INTERACTIVE GRID

MASTER DETAIL PAGE

A Master-Detail page in Oracle APEX is a type of page that allows you to display and manage data from two related tables in a hierarchical manner. It is often used to create user interfaces for scenarios where there is a parent-child relationship between two tables. This type of page is commonly used to represent one-to-many or many-to-many relationships in a database.

Figure 4-1

68

Here's how a Master-Detail page typically works:

Master Section

The "master" section of the page displays records from the parent table. This section often contains a form that allows users to view and interact with the data from the master table. For example, in the current scenario, this section will display data from the Results Master table.

Detail Section

The "detail" section of the page displays records from the child table that are related to the currently selected master record. This section includes an interactive grid, allowing users to view and edit the related data. For example, here you will see marks information from the Results Details table related to a student.

Relationships

The master-detail relationship is established based on a common key between the two tables. This key (RESULT_ID in our scenario) is used to filter and display the relevant detail records based on the selected master record. APEX typically handles the synchronization between the master and detail sections based on user interactions.

Interactivity

Users can interact with the master and detail sections independently. Selecting a record in the master section will automatically update the detail section to show the related data. Users can also add, edit, or delete records in both sections.

Navigation

APEX provides built-in navigation features that allow users to move between master records and see the corresponding detail records without needing to leave the page.

Summary

Creating a Master-Detail page in Oracle APEX involves defining the appropriate data sources, creating an interactive grid component, establishing the master-detail relationship, and configuring the page's behavior and appearance. Master-Detail pages are commonly used in scenarios such as order-entry systems, customer relationship management (CRM) applications, project management tools, and more, where there is a need to display and manage related data in a hierarchical manner.

INTERACTIVE GRID

In Oracle APEX, an Interactive Grid is a powerful component that allows you to create highly interactive and customizable tabular interfaces for viewing, editing, and managing data from a database table or query. When used in a Master-Detail page, Interactive Grids play a significant role in enhancing the user experience and providing advanced functionality for working with both master and detail data.

Here's the role of an Interactive Grid in a Master-Detail page in Oracle APEX:

Detail Data

In a Master-Detail page, the Interactive Grid can be used to display the detail records related to the selected master record. When a user selects a master record in the master section of the page, the Interactive Grid in the detail section can dynamically load and display the corresponding detail records from the related table. This allows users to see all the related data in a tabular format.

Updating Data

Interactive Grids provide inline editing capabilities, which means users can directly edit and update the data within the grid cells without having to navigate to a separate edit form. This is particularly useful for quickly making changes to multiple detail records associated with a master record.

Addition/Deletion

Users can easily add new detail records directly within the Interactive Grid. Additionally, they can delete existing detail records by selecting one or more rows and using the built-in delete functionality.

Sorting/Filtering

Interactive Grids allow users to sort and filter data columns, helping them quickly find the information they need within the detail records.

Pagination

Interactive Grids support pagination, which means large datasets can be divided into smaller chunks, improving performance. The grid can also use lazy loading, where only a subset of data is initially loaded, and more data is fetched as the user scrolls through the grid.

Customization

Interactive Grids offer a wide range of customization options, including column ordering, resizing, reordering, column formatting, highlighting, and more. You can also define computations, validations, and dynamic actions to enhance the behavior and appearance of the grid.

Communication

Interactive Grids can be configured to support communication between the master and detail sections of the page. This means that selecting a record in the master section can automatically update the data displayed in the Interactive Grid within the detail section.

Advanced Features

Interactive Grids can integrate with other APEX components like charts, navigation menus, and more to provide a comprehensive user experience. They can also be designed to support responsive layouts, ensuring a consistent look and feel across different devices.

MASTER/DETAIL TABLES

A master-detail relationship refers to a type of relationship between two tables where one table (the "master" table) contains primary data, and the other table (the "detail" table) contains related data that is linked to the primary data in the master table. This relationship is established using keys, typically through primary key and foreign key constraints. Master-detail relationships are often used to represent one-to-many relationships between two entities.

In this chapter, you will utilize Master/Detail and Interactive Grid components to record students' results. Before creating these pages, you need to set up two tables (Results_Master and Results_Details) to store students' results information. Execute the following steps to create the two tables.

1. From the main SQL Workshop menu, select the first Object Browser option. This action will open the Object Browser page.

2. In the left pane, click the Create Database Objects drop-down list, and select the Table option to create a new table. A new page labeled 'Create Table' will pop up where you will provide definitions of the new table.

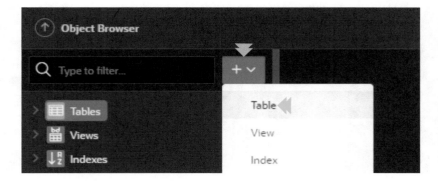

3. Fill in the Create Table form as illustrated in the following figure to create the master table. Use the Edit and Add Column buttons to fill in the columns' details. After completing the table definitions, click the Create Table button.

Figure 4-2

A The RESULT_ID column is the Primary Key in this master table and it will uniquely identify each student's result within the table.

B The STUDENT_ID column is a foreign key in this table and it is added here to create a link between the STUDENTS and RESULTS_MASTER tables. a foreign key is a relational database constraint that establishes a link between two tables based on the values of specified columns. The purpose of a foreign key is to maintain referential integrity between related tables, ensuring that data relationships are consistent and accurate. In this context, only student IDs that are present in the STUDENTS table will be considered valid in the RESULTS_MASTER table.

C The length of the ACADEMIC_SESSION column is 7 and it will store students' session in 9999-99 format – for example, 2023-24.

FOREIGN KEY CONSTRAINT

A foreign key creates a relationship between a column (or set of columns) in a child table and the primary key column(s) in a parent table. This relationship defines a connection between related data. Execute the following steps to create a relationship between the STUDENTS and RESULTS_MASTER tables using a foreign key constraint.

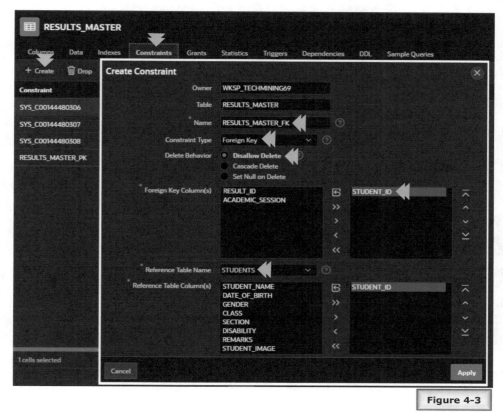

Figure 4-3

4. In Object Browser, click the Constraints tab.

5. Then, click Create option. This action will open the Create Constraint dialog box.

6. Enter RESULTS_MASTER_FK for the foreign key constraint name.

7. Select Foreign Key for the Constraint Type.

8. Select Disallow Delete for Delete Behavior. The default Disallow Delete option will block deletion of rows from the STUDENTS table when they are utilized in the RESULTS_MASTER table.

9. In the Foreign Key Column(s) section, move the STUDENT_ID column to the right pane using the single right-arrow icon (>). This action specifies that the STUDENT_ID column in this table is a foreign key and has a reference in some other table.

10. From the Reference Table Name list, select the STUDENTS table. All columns from this table will appear in the Referenced Table Column(s).

11. From the Reference Table Column(s) pane, move the STUDENT_ID column to the right pane. This action informs APEX that the STUDENT_ID column in the STUDENTS table will be referred to by the STUDENT_ID column in the RESULTS_MASTER table. As a result of this configuration, the two tables establish a relationship centered around the STUDENT_ID column. Click the Apply button.

12. Create the RESULTS_DETAILS table, using the details provided in the following illustration. The table will be used to store the marks that each student has obtained in each subject.

Figure 4-4

A The LINE_NO column will be the Primary Key for this table.

B The RESULT_ID column will act as a foreign key to establish relationship with the RESULTS_MASTER table.

C The SUBJECT column will receive values from the SUBJECTS LOV that was created in Chapter 2.

D The MARKS column will store the obtained marks in the selected subject using the 999 format.

13. Using the Create option in the Constraints tab, create a foreign key constraint as depicted in the following figure to establish a relationship between the RESULTS_MASTER and RESULTS_DETAILS tables. The relationship is created using the RESULT_ID column, which exists in both tables. We selected Cascade Delete for the Delete Behavior attribute. It refers to a feature that allows you to automatically delete related rows in child tables when a row in the parent table is deleted. This helps maintain referential integrity within the database, ensuring that data remains consistent and accurate.

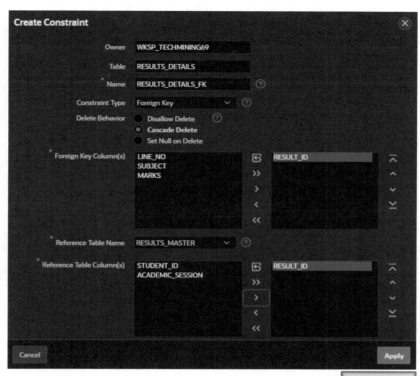

Figure 4-5

The relationship among the three tables you created in this exercise for your application is presented in this diagram.

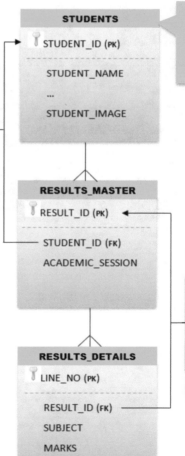

The STUDENT_ID column in the STUDENTS table is a primary key. The same column in the RESULTS_MASTER table acts as a foreign key. This means that every record in the RESULTS_MASTER table must have a corresponding key (STUDENT_ID) in the STUDENTS table.

The RESULT_ID column in the RESULTS_MASTER table is a primary key. The same column in the RESULTS_DETAILS table acts as a foreign key. Which means that every record in the RESULTS_DETAILS table must have a corresponding key (RESULT_ID) in the RESULTS_MASTER table.

CREATE LIST OF VALUES

LOVs help ensure data consistency by providing a predefined set of values for a particular field. Users can only select values from the list, reducing the chance of input errors or typos. This promotes data integrity and accuracy within your application.

You created some list of values in Chapter 2. Here, you will create a couple of LOVs to avoid input errors. Execute the following steps to create one static and one dynamic LOV.

1. Go to Shared Components page. In the Other Components section, click the Lists of Values option. Click the Create button. Then, on the first wizard screen, select the From Scratch option. Enter ACADEMIC SESSION for the LOV name, and set its type to Static. Fill in the Static Values screen as demonstrated in the following figure. Finally, click the Create List of Values button.

Figure 4-6

Now create a dynamic LOV using the following instructions. A Dynamic LOV in Oracle APEX refers to a type of LOV that is generated at runtime based on a SQL query. Unlike a static LOV, where the list of values is predefined and stored within the APEX application, a dynamic LOV generates its list of values from a data source such as a database table, view, web service, or custom logic.

2. On the second wizard screen, enter STUDENTS for the LOV name, and this time select the Dynamic option for the LOV type. Select Local Database and Table for the LOV data source and then select the STUDENTS table. These selections specify that you want to create a dynamic LOV on the STUDENTS table, which is a table in the local database.

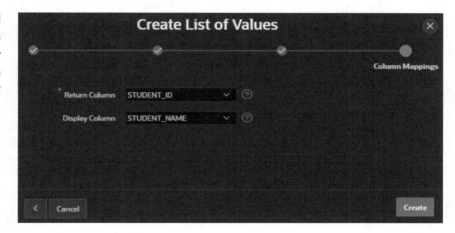

3. On the Column Mappings wizard screen, select STUDENT_ID for Return Column and STUDENT_NAME for Display Column. Click the Create button to complete the dynamic LOV creation process.

Return Column: The Return Column is the column that holds the actual value associated with each LOV option. When a user selects an option from the LOV, the value from the Return Column is what gets stored or returned to the database. It's the underlying data that corresponds to the selected option.

Display Column: The Display Column is the column that holds the human-readable or user-friendly representation of each LOV option. This is the text that users see in the LOV dropdown or other UI elements. The Display Column is what helps users understand and select the desired option from the list.

In many cases, the Return Column and Display Column can be the same column, especially when you want to display and return the same piece of information – as you experienced in all the Static LOVs created so far. However, there are scenarios where you might want to show more descriptive text to the user (Display Column) while storing a corresponding code or ID (Return Column) in the database.

For example, here you're creating an LOV for selecting students:
    Return Column: Student ID (e.g., 101, 102, 103)
    Display Column: Student Name (e.g., Andrew, Mary, Sarah)

In this example, when a user selects "Andrew" from the LOV, the Student ID (101) is what will be stored or used in database operations, but the user sees the more descriptive "Andrew" in the dropdown. This will become clearer once you create some records in the result tables.

Execute the following steps to create the two pages interactively to view and store students' results information.

1. On the application home page, click the Create Page button and then select the Master Detail option on the first wizard screen. On the next wizard screen, select the Drill Down option. A Drill Down master detail contains two pages based on two related tables. The first page contains an interactive report that displays data from the master table. The second page contains two sections – a standard form (to display data from the master table) and an interactive grid (to show information from the details table).

2. On the next wizard screen, fill in the Master Page Definition as illustrated here. The master page is typically the starting point of the interaction. It often contains a list or a report displaying summarized data (e.g., a list of orders or students). Users can select a record from this list, and upon selection, the associated detail page is displayed. The data source defined for the master page retrieves data from the RESULTS_MASTER table. This data is used in an interactive report to display the list of records from the master table, allowing users to select a record for further details. Click Next to proceed.

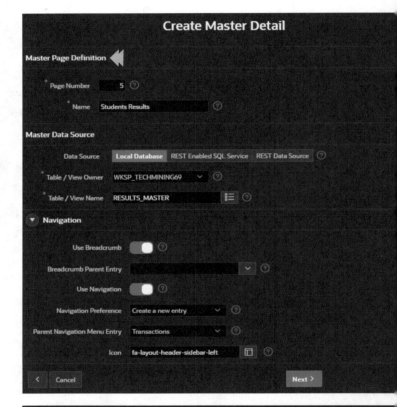

3. The next wizard screen will automatically populate the Primary Key column – RESULT_ID. From the Form Navigation Order list, select the RESULT_ID column. After creation, the form page will have next and previous buttons for navigation among students' results. The values from the RESULT_ID column will be used to navigate among records. When users are viewing or editing detail records in a Master/Detail setup and there are multiple records to navigate through, the Form Navigation Order property determines the order in which focus is shifted among different records as users click the "Next" or "Previous" buttons. This property ensures that users can seamlessly move between different records' detail information without having to manually select one from the interactive report. Click Next.

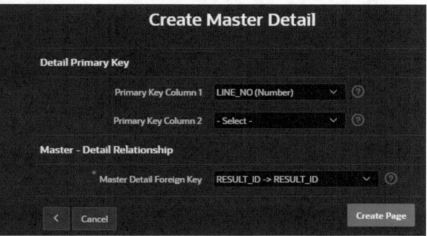

4. Fill in the Detail Page Definition form as illustrated here. On this wizard screen you specify that result details on the details page (Page 6) will be shown from the RESULTS_DETAILS table. Click Next.

5. On this final wizard screen, the LINE_NO column is selected automatically as the primary key column for the RESULTS_DETAILS table. For Master Detail Foreign Key, select RESULT_ID -> RESULT_ID from the adjacent list. This value specifies the column that creates the relationship between the master and detail tables. Recall that both master and detail tables have the RESULT_ID column that creates a relationship between the two tables, and which controls display of correct related detail records during navigation. Click Create Page to complete this process.

Prior to executing these pages, let's examine the wizard's contributions. The master page (Page 5) has been generated, featuring an Interactive Report that will present a list of students' results from the RESULTS_MASTER table. On the other hand, the details page (Page 6) holds numerous elements waiting to be unveiled. This section delves into all the components that the wizard autonomously crafted for Page 6, equipping it with comprehensive functionalities to efficiently manage this module. Note that most of the components created here on Page 6 were discussed in the last chapter. This section will elaborate on the components new to this page.

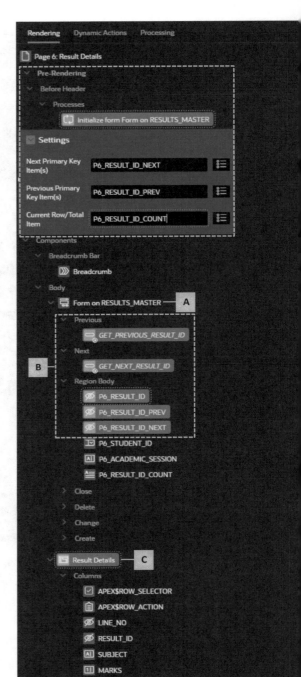

A   Form Region: The Form on RESULTS_MASTER region is a Form type region and it displays master information like Result ID, Student ID, and Academic Session in page items from the RESULTS_MASTER table.

B   GET_PREVIOUS_RESULT_ID and GET_NEXT_RESULT_ID Buttons: These buttons are added to the master region to fetch previous and next results, respectively. For example, when you click the Next button, the page is submitted to get the next result from the server by triggering the Initialize Form on RESULTS_MASTER process (defined under the Pre-Rendering node) using the value set for Next Primary Key Item(s) property in this process. The Next Primary Key Item(s) and Previous Primary Key Item(s) properties in this process are associated with respective hidden page items to fetch next and previous result ids. Based on the currently fetched result id, which is held in the page item P6_RESULT_ID, the process dynamically obtains the next and previous result ids and stores them in two hidden page items: P6_RESULT_ID_NEXT and P6_RESULT_ID_PREV. Hidden items are form elements (such as text fields, checkboxes, or other input elements) that are included on a page but are not visible to the user when the page is rendered. These items are used to store and manage data behind the scenes, without the need for the user to interact with them directly. The visibility of the Next and Previous buttons is controlled by a Server-side Condition (Item is NOT NULL), which says that these buttons will be visible only when their corresponding hidden items have some values. If you make any modification to an order on Page 6 and navigate to another order record using any of these buttons, the changes are saved to the two database tables. This is because the Action property of the two buttons is set to Submit Page. When the page is submitted, two processes (Process Form on RESULTS_MASTER and Result Details - Save Interactive Grid Data defined later in this section) are executed to make the changes permanent.

C   Result Details: This is an Interactive Grid region, which is generated to view, add, modify, and delete subjects and marks. The information you provided in this interactive grid is saved to the RESULTS_DETAILS table through a process named Result Details - Save Interactive Grid Data – discussed next.

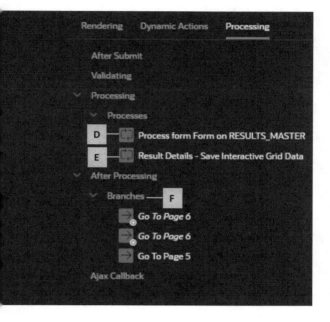

D Process Form: This Automatic Row Processing (DML) type process is generated by the wizard to handle DML operations performed on the master row of a result, which gets into the RESULTS_MASTER table. It comes into action when you click Delete, Save, or Create buttons. This process and the actions associated with the three buttons were previously explained in the preceding chapter.

E Save Interactive Grid Data: This process is responsible to handle DML operations on the details table (RESULTS_DETAILS). It is a predefined built-in process that is automatically available when you use an Interactive Grid component on a page. This process is designed to handle the saving of data that has been edited, added, or deleted within an Interactive Grid region. The primary purpose of this process is to manage the changes made to the data displayed in an Interactive Grid and persist those changes to the database. This process is typically triggered when the user interacts with the Interactive Grid, such as modifying cell values, adding new rows, or deleting existing rows. The process analyzes the changes made in the Interactive Grid and generates the necessary SQL statements to update, insert, or delete records in the underlying database table(s).

F Branches: Branches are components used to control the flow of an application based on user actions or specific conditions. They allow you to define what happens next when a user interacts with a page, clicks a button, or encounters a specific situation. Essentially, branches determine the navigation and behavior of your application.

When you submit a page, the Oracle APEX server receives a submission request and executes the associated processes and validations. Following this, the server determines the destination within the application using the defined branches. By default, the current page is selected as the target. For instance, when using the Next or Previous buttons on Page 6, you remain on that same page. However, if you wish to direct users to a different page, you can achieve this by creating branches.

In the current context, clicking any button other than Next or Previous on Page 6 redirects you back to Page 5. A branch encompasses two crucial properties: Behavior and Server-side Condition. The Behavior section specifies the destination page (or URL) to redirect to, while the Condition section determines when the branch is activated.

In this scenario, the first two branches are configured to keep you on Page 6, corresponding to the Next and Previous buttons. You can find these configurations in the 'When Button Pressed' properties of these branches. The third branch, however, guides you back to Page 5 when any other button on the page is clicked. This behavior is defined in the Behavior section, which specifies the redirection.

Execute the following steps to associate LOVs you created in this chapter and modify some page components.

1. Open page 6. Click the form region "Form on RESULTS_MASTER" and set its title to Result Information. Expand the Region Body node under the Form region. Click the P6_STUDENT_ID page item and set the adjacent properties. Here, we used Popup LOV instead of Select List. In Oracle APEX, both Select Lists and Popup LOVs are used to provide users with a list of options to choose from, but they have some differences in terms of functionality and user interface. Select Lists are best for providing a compact list of options that are visible directly on the page, while Popup LOVs are ideal for situations where there are many options and the ability to search and filter is beneficial. The choice between the two depends on the specific user interface requirements and the number of options you need to present to users.

PROPERTY	VALUE
Type	Popup LOV
Label	Student
Display As	Modal Dialog
Type (List of Values)	Shared Component
List of Values	STUDENTS
Display Extra Values	Turn Off
Display Null Value	Turn Off

2. Click the P6_ACADEMIC_SESSION item and set the adjacent properties. Since the Academic Sessions LOV comprises just three values, we chose to display this item as a Select List.

PROPERTY	VALUE
Type	Select List
Type (List of Values)	Shared Component
List of Values	ACADEMIC SESSIONS
Display Extra Values	Turn Off

3. Expand the columns node under the Result Details Interactive Grid region. Click the SUBJECT column and set the adjacent properties for this column. At runtime, the column will be displayed as a Select List containing the subjects using the SUBJECTS LOV. Note that this LOV was created in Chapter 2.

PROPERTY	VALUE
Type	Select List
Type (List of Values)	Shared Component
List of Values	SUBJECTS
Display Extra Values	Turn Off

4. Click the Result Details Interactive Grid region. In the Property Editor, scroll down to the Server-side Condition section, and remove the condition (Item is NOT NULL) by choosing the – Select – placeholder for the Type property. The default condition you just removed displays the interactive grid only when you modify an existing record. For new record, the interactive grid is hidden. By removing the default condition, the interactive grid becomes visible for new results as well. Click the Save button to preserve the changes.

PROPERTY	VALUE
Type (Server-side Condition)	- Select -

5. Under the Processing tab, click the Save Interactive Grid Data process and set the following properties. We switched the process default type to Execute Code. In this code, we specified SQL Insert, Update, and Delete statements to manually handle the three operations for the Interactive Grid data. The :APEX$ROW_STATUS is a built-in substitution string, which is used to refer to the row status in an Interactive Grid. This placeholder returns the status of 'C' if created, 'U' if updated, or 'D' if deleted for the currently processed interactive grid row. In the Editable Region property, we select the interactive grid region (Result Details) to associate with this process. An "Editable Region" is a region type that allows users to input or edit data directly on a page. Editable regions are often used in forms, and interactive grids to provide a user interface for data manipulation. They allow users to interact with the data and make changes, and these changes can be processed and saved to the database.

PROPERTY	VALUE
Type	Execute Code
Editable Region	Result Details

PL/SQL Code	begin
	  case :APEX$ROW_STATUS
	  when 'C' then
	    insert into RESULTS_DETAILS
	      (line_no, result_id, subject, marks) values (null, :P6_RESULT_ID, :SUBJECT, :MARKS);
	  when 'U' then
	    update RESULTS_DETAILS
	      set subject = :SUBJECT,
	      marks = :MARKS
	      where line_no = :LINE_NO and result_id = :RESULT_ID;
	  when 'D' then
	    delete from RESULTS_DETAILS
	      where line_no = :LINE_NO and result_id = :RESULT_ID;
	  end case;
	end;

6. Switch back to the Rendering tab on page 6. Press and hold the control key on your keyboard and click the Cancel, Delete, Save, and Create buttons. In the Layout section in Property Editor, set the Position property to Copy. This change will place the four buttons at the top of the page. Save your work.

NOTE

Before replacing the default interactive grid process with the provided PL/SQL code, I conducted tests on the record insertion process. During testing, I observed that the data I entered in the master section was successfully saved, and the RESULT_ID in the master table was automatically generated. However, upon examining the details table, I discovered that the RESULT_ID column contained null values in all rows. Despite having established the proper relationship between the master and detail pages during their creation, I was unable to determine the cause of this issue. The absence of RESULT_ID information in the details table resulted in a broken relationship, causing only the master record to be visible, with no subject or marks information displayed in the interactive grid. Consequently, I implemented the aforementioned PL/SQL code as a workaround.

TEST THE MODULE

Run the application and select the Students Results option from the application menu. Page 5 with an empty interactive report will come up. Click the Create button on this page. The form page (Page 6) will open.

Fill in the form page as illustrated in the adjacent figure. In the master section, select Andrew from the Student Popup LOV. Then, select First Session from the Academic Session list. Double click the first empty row in the detail section to enable it. In the Subject column, select subjects and enter marks for each subject. Use the Add Row button to add rows for additional subjects. After completing the form, click the Create button. The result data will be saved and you will be taken back to the interactive report page showing Andrew's result.

As you can see, we entered 200 in the Marks column for the Computer result, which is an error. In the next section, we will learn the use of validations to overcome such errors.

Andrew's result data will be displayed in the interactive report page. You can use the edit icon being displayed in the first column to open and view the result details on the form page.

Note the tiny red triangles at top-left on Student Id and Academic Session page items. The red triangle indicator in Oracle APEX page items at runtime is associated with mandatory table columns in your database schema. When a column in your database table is marked as "mandatory" (also known as "not null"), Oracle APEX will automatically recognize this information and apply the red triangle indicator to the corresponding page item in the application's forms by applying 'Required - Floating' value to the Template property. The red triangle serves as a visual cue to users that the data in the associated page item must be filled out before the form can be successfully submitted and the data can be saved to the database.

It's part of the user interface design in Oracle APEX to enhance user experience and ensure that they don't miss any essential fields when filling out a form. So, if you have a mandatory table column, you will likely see the red triangle next to the corresponding page item on any forms that allow data input or modification for that table. The aforementioned Template property is used in conjunction with the Value Required property to validate a page item.

Add two more sets of result information using the details provided in the following table, and utilize the two navigation buttons (as illustrated in figure 4-1) to navigate among the three results you have created so far.

MASTER		DETAILS			
STUDENT	ACADEMIC SESSION	ENGLISH	MATHS	PHYSICS	COMPUTER
Mary	First Session	75	82	68	92
Sarah	First Session	69	95	84	63

CREATE VALIDATION

Validation refers to the process of checking user-input data against predefined criteria to ensure its accuracy, integrity, and compliance with business rules before it is processed or stored in the database. Validations help prevent incorrect or inconsistent data from entering the system, thereby maintaining data quality and reliability.

Oracle APEX provides several types of validations that you can create and apply to various components like page items, interactive grid columns, and other user input elements. In this task, you will create a validation on the Marks column to store valid values.

1. Open Page 6 in Page Designer and click the Processing tab. Right-click the Validating node, and select Create Validation from the context menu. Set the following properties for the validation.

2. After creating the validation, test it by using null, zero, and 200 for Andrew's computer marks. Finally set Andrew's computer marks to 100.

PROPERTY	VALUE
Name	Validate Marks
Editable Region	Result Details
Type	Function Body (returning Error Text)
Language	PL/SQL

PL/SQL Function Body Returning Error Text	IF :MARKS IS NULL or :MARKS = 0 THEN
	        RETURN 'Marks should not be null or zero';
	ELSIF :MARKS > 100 THEN
	        RETURN 'Marks should be less than 100';
	ELSE
	        RETURN NULL; -- Validation successful
	END IF;

Type (Server-side Condition)	Request is contained in value
Value	CREATE,SAVE

When setting up validations in Oracle APEX, you typically associate them with specific items (page items or interactive grid columns) within the editable region. When it comes to validation, the concept of an "Editable Region" might refer to specifying the region in which the validation should take place. For example, if you have an editable region like a form or an interactive grid, you can define validation rules that are specific to the data entered or edited within that region.

For instance, in the context of an editable region, you might have validations like:
- Checking if required fields are filled out.
- Verifying that numeric values are within a certain range.
- Ensuring that a start date is before an end date.
- Validating that an email address has the correct format.

These validations are performed on the data within the editable region to ensure its accuracy and integrity before it's saved to the database.

Applying validation to an interactive grid column in Oracle APEX involves creating validation rules that define the conditions under which data in the grid column is considered valid. You can apply various types of validations, such as PL/SQL, JavaScript, or SQL. In the current scenario, we applied the PL/SQL validation, which is a type of validation that allows you to define custom PL/SQL code that will be executed to validate the data in the MARKS column using the :MARKS bind variable.

A bind variable is a placeholder that is used to dynamically pass values to SQL queries, PL/SQL code, and other database operations. Instead of directly embedding values into your SQL statements or code, you use bind variables to bind the values at runtime, which offers several advantages, including security and performance. Using bind variables helps protect your application against SQL injection attacks. Bind variables prevent user input from being directly substituted into SQL queries, reducing the risk of malicious code execution. Bind variables can also improve query performance by allowing the database to cache execution plans more effectively. This is especially true in cases where the same SQL query is executed multiple times with different parameter values. In this code, :MARKS is a bind variable that represents the value entered by the user in the MARKS column. At runtime, the bind variable is replaced with the actual value from the column when the code is executed.

The provided PL/SQL code is another validation logic snippet intended to validate the value of in the MARKS column within an Oracle APEX application. This code ensures that the entered value for the MARKS column adheres to specific criteria. Let's break down the code step by step:

IF :MARKS IS NULL or :MARKS = 0 THEN checks if the value of :MARKS is either null or equal to 0. If this condition evaluates to true, the code inside the corresponding THEN block is executed: RETURN 'Marks should not be null or zero'; This line returns an error message indicating that the "Marks" value should not be left blank or set to zero.

ELSIF :MARKS > 100 THEN checks if the value of ':MARKS' is greater than 100. If this condition evaluates to true, the code inside the THEN block is executed: RETURN 'Marks should be less than 100'; This line returns an error message indicating that the "Marks" value should be less than 100.

If none of the above conditions are met, then the code inside the ELSE block is executed. RETURN NULL; is used to indicate that the validation has passed successfully. Returning NULL from a validation function signifies that no validation error occurred.

In summary, this code snippet checks whether the value entered in the MARKS column is null, zero, or greater than 100. Depending on the outcome of these conditions, it returns corresponding error messages or indicates successful validation. This type of PL/SQL validation can be attached to a page item or a column in Oracle APEX to ensure that the data entered by users aligns with specific business rules and validation criteria before proceeding further.

WHAT YOU LEARNED

A Master-Detail page in Oracle APEX is a type of page that allows you to display related data from two or more tables in a hierarchical manner. It's commonly used to display parent-child relationships, such as orders and order items, customers and their contacts, or any scenario where you have data with a one-to-many or many-to-one relationship. Here's a summarized list of key points about Master-Detail pages that you learned in this chapter:

- **Relationship:** A Master-Detail page displays data from two or more related tables where there is a parent-child relationship based on common columns.

- **Parent Table:** The parent table typically represents the "master" data or the main record, while the child table holds the "detail" records associated with the parent.

- **Page Structure:** A Master-Detail page often consists of a form region displaying the master (parent) data and a nested interactive grid region displaying the related detail (child) data.

- **Linking Columns:** The tables are linked using columns that establish the relationship. These columns are often foreign keys in the child table referencing the primary key in the parent table.

- **Interactive Grids:** Interactive Grids are commonly used to display detail data. They allow users to interactively view, filter, sort, and edit data.

- **Parent-Child Communication:** APEX provides built-in mechanisms to enable communication between the master and detail regions, such as selecting a master row to display corresponding detail data.

- **Data Integrity:** Master-Detail pages help maintain data integrity by enforcing relationships and providing a clear way to manage related records.

- **Editing and CRUD Operations:** Users can edit, insert, and delete data in both the master and detail regions, allowing for comprehensive data management.

- **Validation and Processing:** You can apply validations and processing to both master and detail data, ensuring that data meets specific criteria before being saved.

- **Wizard Creation:** Oracle APEX provides wizards to streamline the creation of Master-Detail pages, making it easier to set up relationships and regions.

Overall, Master-Detail pages are essential in creating rich and interactive applications that effectively manage and present hierarchical data relationships. They provide a structured way to display and interact with related records, making it easier for users to navigate and manage their data.

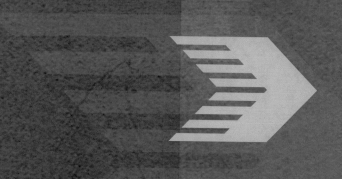

5

ACTIONS MENU

ABOUT ACTIONS MENU

In Oracle APEX, an "Actions" menu in the context of Interactive Report and Interactive Grid refers to a customizable menu that allows users to perform various actions on the displayed data within these components. It provides a convenient way to interact with the data and access different functionalities without cluttering the main interface.

Figure 5-1

The Actions menu typically appears as a button or icon near the top of the report. When clicked, it opens a dropdown menu containing a list of predefined actions or options that users can choose from. These actions can include tasks such as sorting, filtering, exporting data, saving customized report settings, and more.

The key difference between the Interactive Report and Interactive Grid Actions menu lies in the purpose and functionality of these components. The Interactive Grid's Actions menu is geared toward managing and editing tabular data, while the Interactive Report's Actions menu focuses on data presentation, filtering, sorting, and exporting. The choice between using an Interactive Grid or an Interactive Report depends on the specific requirements of the application and the nature of the data being displayed.

Some common actions that might be available in the Actions menu include:

Column Sorting

Allowing users to sort the data in the report by specific columns in ascending or descending order.

Resetting Report

Giving users the ability to reset any applied filters and sorting, returning the report to its default state.

Column Filtering

Enabling users to apply filters to one or more columns to refine the displayed data.

Row Selection

Users can select one or multiple rows for further actions.

Exporting Data

Providing options to export the report data to formats like CSV, Excel, PDF, etc.

Editing Mode

Switching between read-only and editable modes for rows.

Saving Report

Allowing users to save their customized column layouts, filters, and other settings for future use.

Row Actions

Customizable actions that can be performed on specific rows, such as editing, deleting, or executing custom logic.

The Actions menu offers users a way to interact with the data by providing a dropdown menu with various options for sorting, filtering, exporting, and customizing the behavior, and it enhances the user experience and usability of these two import components.

Before delving into the intricacies of the Actions menu, take a moment to incorporate some results data using the table provided below. This will provide you with a comprehensive grasp of the array of options available within the Actions menu.

You have already added the first three records shown in the following table. So, add the remaining six records using the master/detail page created in the previous chapter.

	MASTER		DETAILS			
	STUDENT	ACADEMIC SESSION	ENGLISH	MATHS	PHYSICS	COMPUTER
1	Andrew	First Session	100	100	100	100
2	Mary	First Session	75	82	68	92
3	Sarah	First Session	69	95	84	63
4	Andrew	Second Session	78	56	25	64
5	Mary	Second Session	71	29	56	84
6	Sarah	Second Session	65	46	28	73
7	Andrew	Third Session	84	65	48	97
8	Mary	Third Session	64	86	76	53
9	Sarah	Third Session	84	98	85	76

CUSTOMIZE REPORT SOURCE

If you're dealing with more complex scenarios or need to completely change the underlying data source behavior, you can handle it easily. Oracle APEX provides a versatile platform, and you can achieve a lot of customization using SQL, PL/SQL, Web Sources, and various processes. In this section, you will learn how to change the default data source of an interactive report.

Execute the following steps to change the default data source of the interactive report, which is the RESULTS_MASTER table. You will replace the default data source with a custom SQL query that fetches data from three tables: STUDENTS, RESULTS_MASTER, and RESULTS_DETAILS.

1. Open the Students Results page (Page 5) in page designer.

2. Click the Students Results Interactive Report region, and change the Type property under the Source section from Table/View to SQL Query. Enter the following query in the SQL Query box. The query is available in the book's source. After entering this query and exiting the SQL Query box, the columns under the 'Students Results' interactive region will update to match the columns specified in the query.

    The SQL Query will fetch data from the three tables mentioned above. The last column in the SELECT query, SUM(RD.MARKS), sums up the marks of all subjects by each result to show the aggregate marks obtained by each student per academic session.

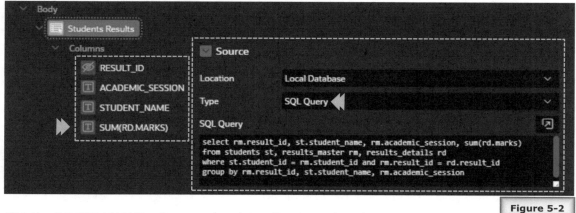

Figure 5-2

3. Click the SUM(RD.MARKS) column, and set it heading to Total Marks.

    If you save and run the page, the interactive report will show just one column, 'Academic Session', from the query. Execute the next step to show the other hidden columns using the Actions menu.

1. **Show Columns:** Click the ACTIONS MENU. Select the first Columns option. In the Select Columns dialog box, move the Student Name and Total Marks columns from the 'Do Not Display' section to the 'Display in Report' section using the arrow keys shown between the two panes. Then, arrange the columns as demonstrated in the adjacent figure using the arrow keys provided on the right side. After making these modifications, click the Apply button to save the changes. All three columns will become visible on the interactive report page.

2. **Sort Data:** Again, click the ACTIONS MENU. Select the Sort option from the Data menu. In the Sort dialog box, choose Academic Session as the first sorting column, followed by the Student Name column. Leave the Directions of these columns set to the default Ascending option. Click the Apply button to save the changes. The results data on the interactive report will be sorted first by the Academic Session column, and then by the Student Name column. If you want to change the sort to some other order, open the Sort dialog box again and select the columns as you wish.

3. **Save Report:** Click the Actions menu and then select Save Report from the Report menu. In the Save Report dialog box, select As Default Report Settings from the Save list. Then, select Primary for Default Report Type, and click Apply. Make sure to consistently save a report using the Actions menu after making any alterations. Failing to do so will result in your changes not being visible the next time you access the application. Interactive Reports offer filters, highlights, and customizations, which Oracle APEX can remember for automatic future use. Users can create multiple reports based on this default primary report, as explained later.

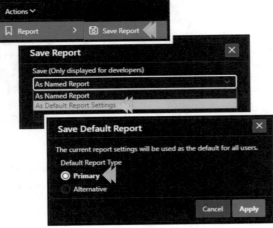

ALTERNATIVE REPORT

In Oracle APEX, an alternative report typically refers to a secondary or backup report that provides an alternative view of data or information. It serves as an additional option for presenting data, often with different formatting, grouping, sorting, or filtering compared to the primary or default report. Alternative reports are commonly used to offer users diverse ways of visualizing and analyzing data without altering the main report's configuration. This can be especially useful when users have varying preferences for how they want to interact with and interpret the data presented in an application.

In this segment, you'll create an Alternative Report named 'Sessions Review' derived from the default primary report. This alternative view will be presented with a distinct layout achieved by utilizing the Control Break utility on the Academic Session column. Follow the steps outlined below on the primary interactive report to generate the Alternate report.

4. With the default primary report displayed on the interactive report page, choose the Save Report option from the Actions menu – see Step 3. Then, select the As Default Report Settings option. Now, select the Alternative option, enter Sessions Review for the report name, and click the Apply button. The next set of steps will be performed on the new alternative report, so, from the reports list, select the Sessions Review alternative report.

5. **Control Break:** From the Actions menu, select Control Break under the Format menu. Then, choose the Academic Session column, and click Apply. The Control Break functionality allows you to incorporate grouping into your report using one or multiple columns. The Column attribute specifies the column for grouping, while the Status attribute determines the activation of the control break. When you click the Apply button, you will see the report results are grouped by the Academic Session column and the Control Break column rule is listed under the toolbar. A checkbox is displayed next to the Control Break column and it is used to turn the control break rule on or off. The control break can be removed from the report by clicking on the small cross icon that appears next to the Academic Session control break.

6. **Highlight Row:** Select Highlight from the Format menu. Enter Marks 300 And Above in the Name box. Select Row for Highlight Type. Keep the Enabled switch turned on. Select background and text colors using the color picker. In the Highlight Condition section at the bottom, select Total Marks for Column, >= (greater than or equal to) for operator, and enter 300 in the Expression box. Click the Apply button. Oracle APEX offers a conditional highlighting feature within interactive reports to emphasize significant data amidst the rest. Through the highlight feature in the Actions menu, users can exhibit data using diverse colors contingent on specific conditions. It's possible to establish numerous highlight conditions for a report. In this particular step, the directive is to emphasize all rows in the report with a light green background and dark green text whenever the value within the Total Marks column is greater than or equal to 300. Any rows meeting this condition will be highlighted with the designated colors. To modify an existing highlight rule, simply click on its entry in the interactive report toolbar, as shown at the top of this figure.

7. **Highlight Cell:** Create another highlight rule as illustrated in the adjacent figure. This rule is similar to the previous one with different parameters. In contrast to the previous action, where complete rows were highlighted, this one highlight individual cells with red background and white text color and applies it to all cells in the report where the Total Marks are below 250.

After applying the Control Break and the two highlight rules, the outcome of the Session Review report should resemble the visual representation depicted in the figure below.

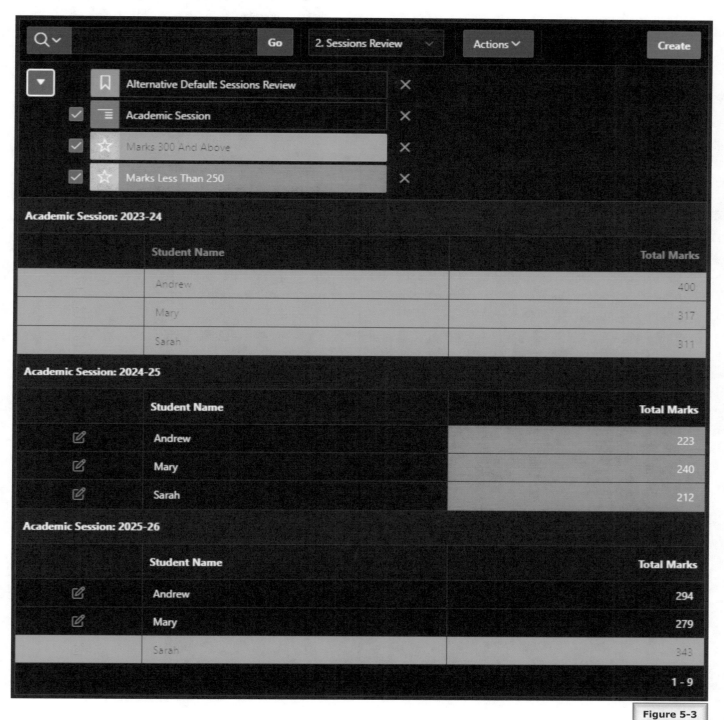

8. **Chart:** Select Chart from the Actions menu and then select the options as illustrated in the adjacent figure. You can generate charts in Interactive Reports based on the results of a report. You can specify the type of chart together with the data in the report you want to chart. In this step, you are creating a horizontal bar chart to showcase student marks by each academic session. The chart will employ academic sessions as labels and the sum of marks as values.

The chart's appearance should resemble the illustration provided below. Observe that the toolbar now incorporates two icons: "View Report" and "View Chart." If the chart does not display, click on the "View Chart" icon within the toolbar. Hover your cursor over each bar to display the total marks for each session.

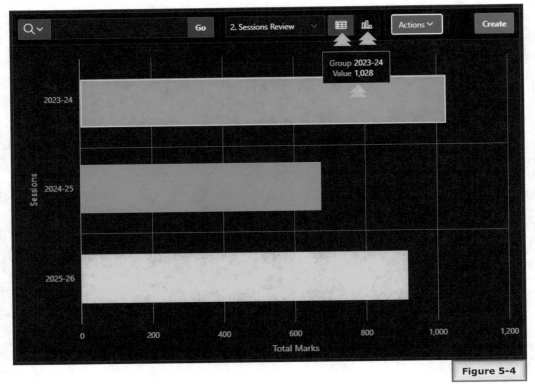

Figure 5-4

9. **Group By:** Click the View Report icon in the interactive report toolbar to switch back to the report view interface. Select the Group By option in the Actions menu. Set the properties as show in the adjacent figure and click Apply. Use the Add Function button to add the second function (Average). The first function calculates the sum of marks, while the second function calculates the average marks. By using the Group By feature in the Actions menu, you can effectively transform a regular report into a summarized and structured view of your data. This is especially useful when you want to present aggregated information and provide users with the ability to navigate through the summarized data to access detailed records.

10. Click Actions ➔ Report ➔ Save Report. Select As Default Report Setting from the Save list. Select Alternative for the Default Report Type. The Name box should display Sessions Review. Click Apply. A new icon labeled 'View Group By' will be added to the toolbar, and this view will resemble the following illustration.

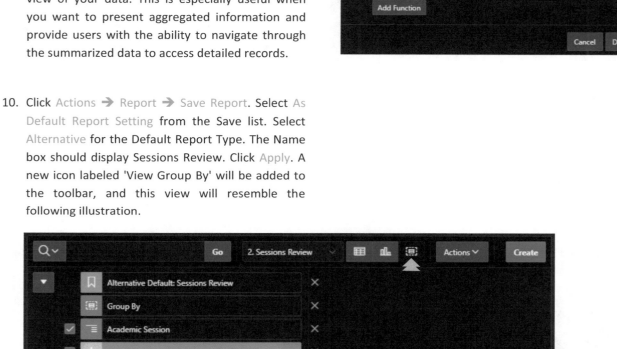

Figure 5-5

99

PRIVATE REPORT

A private report refers to a type of report that is specific to an individual user. Private reports are tied to the preferences of individual users. Each user can create, modify, and manage their own private reports without affecting other users' reports. Users can tailor private reports to their specific needs. They can choose columns, apply sorting and filtering, and adjust the report's appearance based on their preferences. Private reports are generally visible only to the user who created them. They are not shared by default with other users of the application.

In the previous segment, you created an Alternative Report based on academic sessions. In this segment, you'll create a Private Report named 'Students Review,' and all the views in this report will focus on students and their marks.

1. Select the default Primary Report from the Reports drop-down list in the toolbar. From the Actions menu, select Save Report. From the Save drop-down list, select As Named Report. For report Name, enter Students Review, and click the Apply button. A new Private report group will be added to the reports list in the toolbar, carrying a new report named Students Review. When you click the Apply button, the new private report is displayed on your screen.

2. **Control Break**: With the Students Review report displayed on your screen, click Actions ➔ Format ➔ Control Break. In the first row under 'Column,' select Student Name, set 'Status' to Enabled, and then click Apply.

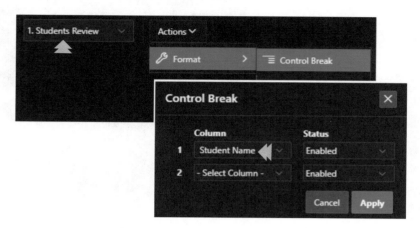

This is the output after applying the Control Break. In the previous exercise, the control break was applied to academic sessions. In this case, it is focusing on students.

Figure 5-6

3. **Chart**: Click Actions ➜ Chart. Set parameters for the chart as illustrated in the adjacent figure. Click the Apply button to create the chart.

The chart uses the Average function (as compared to the Sum function used in the previous exercise). Andrew has secured 917 marks in his three sessions. The average for this student comes to 305.667 (917/3) and this is what you see when you move your mouse over the bar representing Andrew.

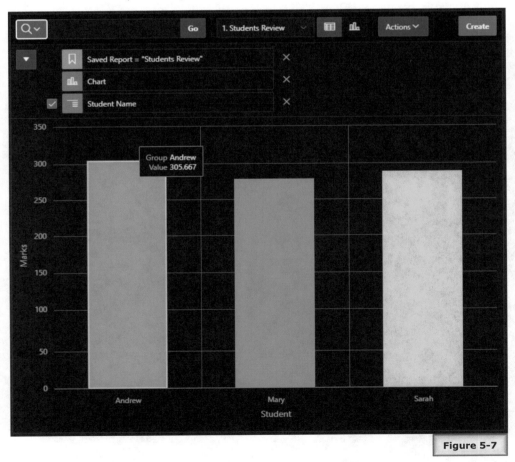

Figure 5-7

4. **Group By**: Click the View Report icon to switch back. Click Actions ➔ Group By. Set the parameters for this view as shown in the adjacent figure. Turn on the Sum switch for all three functions to display grand totals. Save the report.

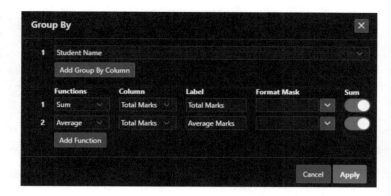

This is the output of the Group By view. In this view, you have applied the Sum and Average functions to the Total Marks column. This allows you to display both the total marks secured by each student in all three sessions and their respective averages.

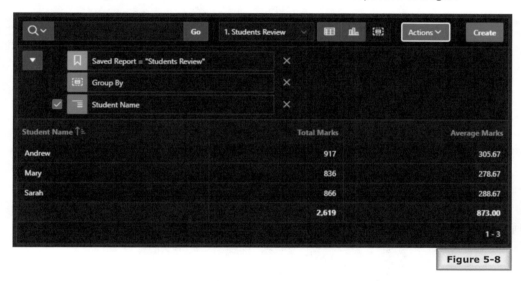

Figure 5-8

5. **Pivot View**: Click the View Report icon. Click Actions ➔ Pivot. Set parameters as show in the adjacent figure. Don't forget to turn on the Sum switch to show grand totals on the page. Save the report.

This is the output of the Pivot view. In Oracle APEX, a Pivot View is a feature that allows you to transform a regular tabular report into a pivot table. A pivot table presents data in a cross-tabular format, summarizing and aggregating values based on specified dimensions and measures. With the Pivot View feature in Oracle APEX, you can dynamically reorganize and summarize your data. You define rows, columns, and measures, and the pivot table automatically aggregates data based on those criteria. This can be very useful for data analysis and reporting when you want to see data from different angles.

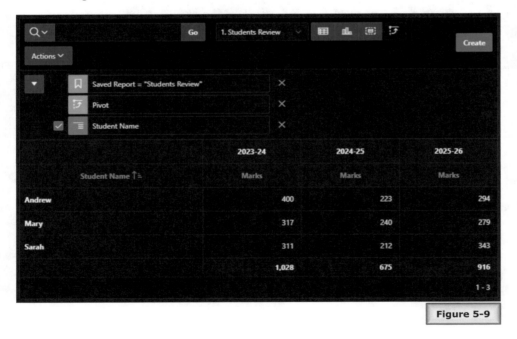

Figure 5-9

6. **Search Data**: The Search box in the toolbar allows users to perform keyword-based searches within the report's data to quickly locate specific records that match their search terms. In the accompanying illustration, I entered andrew into the search box and clicked the Go button. As a result, the report was filtered to show only records related to Andrew. To remove this filter, click the cross icon next to the filter titled Row text contains 'andrew.'

7. **Filter**: The Filter option allows users to apply specific filtering criteria to the report's data. This option is used to dynamically refine the data displayed in the report, focusing only on the records that meet the selected criteria. In the filtering interface, users can specify the criteria they want to use for filtering. This involves selecting columns, defining conditions (e.g., greater than, equal to, etc.), and entering values. In this example, a filter is applied to show records related to the academic session 2025-26.

I have created the following Pivot Table within a new Interactive Report using the query provided below. This Pivot Table displays the details of marks secured by each student in each session.

```
SELECT st.student_name, rm.academic_session, rd.subject, rd.marks
FROM    students st, results_master rm, results_details rd
WHERE st.student_id = rm.student_id and rm.result_id = rd.result_id
```

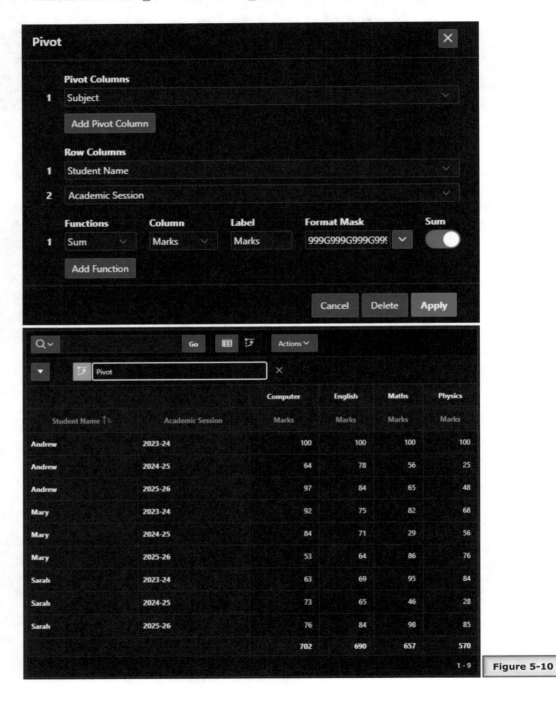

Student Name ↑≡	Academic Session	Computer Marks	English Marks	Maths Marks	Physics Marks
Andrew	2023-24	100	100	100	100
Andrew	2024-25	64	78	56	25
Andrew	2025-26	97	84	65	48
Mary	2023-24	92	75	82	68
Mary	2024-25	84	71	29	56
Mary	2025-26	53	64	86	76
Sarah	2023-24	63	69	95	84
Sarah	2024-25	73	65	46	28
Sarah	2025-26	76	84	98	85
		702	690	657	570

1 - 9   **Figure 5-10**

The Download option in the Actions menu of an Interactive Report allows users to export the data displayed in the report to various formats, facilitating offline access, analysis, and sharing of the data. This feature enhances the usability of the report and provides users with the ability to work with the data in different applications. Common download formats that users might be able to choose from include CSV, Excel, and PDF. The CSV option allows users to download the report data in Comma-Separated Values (CSV) format. CSV is a commonly used format for data interchange and can be opened in spreadsheet applications like Microsoft Excel. The Excel option lets users download the report data in Excel format. The PDF option enables users to download the report data in Portable Document Format (PDF). By turning on the 'Send as Email' switch, you can specify an email address to send the report. The recipient will receive the report as an attachment. The Subscription option in the Actions menu allows you to do the same. Users can subscribe to an interactive report to receive the report in email as attachment when the report is updated.

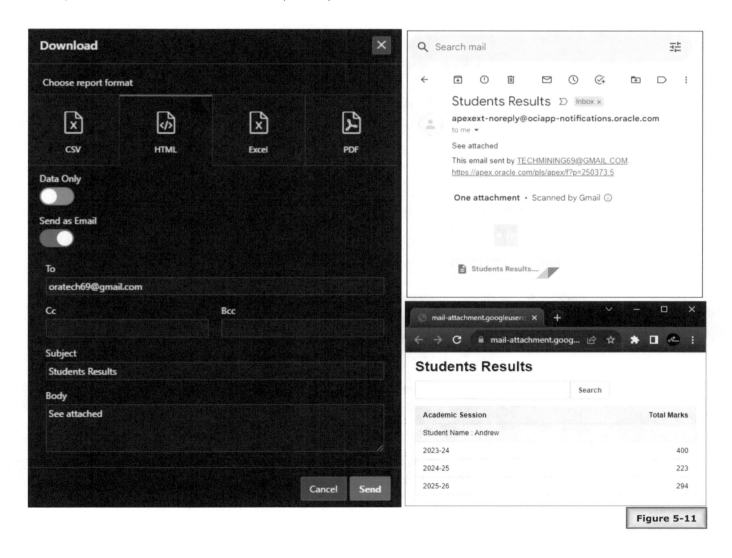

Figure 5-11

WHAT YOU LEARNED

The Actions Menu in Oracle APEX refers to a feature within Interactive Reports and Interactive Grids, which are dynamic and customizable data presentation components used to display and interact with data retrieved from a database. The Actions Menu provides users with a set of options that they can perform on the data displayed. Here is a summary of the features within the Actions menu that you've explored in this chapter:

- **Column Selection:** Enables users to choose which columns are displayed in the report, customizing their view.

- **Sorting:** Allows users to sort the data in ascending or descending order based on selected columns.

- **Control Break:** The Control Break functionality allows you to incorporate grouping into your report using one or multiple columns.

- **Highlighting:** Allows users to highlight specific cells or rows based on conditions or criteria.

- **Chart:** Display data in a chart for visual analysis.

- **Aggregations:** Provides options to perform calculations like sum, average, count, etc., on selected columns.

- **Download:** Provides options for users to download the displayed data in various formats, such as CSV, Excel, PDF, etc., for offline use or further analysis.

- **Save Report:** It allows users to save their customized view settings and configurations of the current report. This feature is particularly useful when users want to preserve specific filter settings, column ordering, sorting preferences, and other customization options so that they can quickly access the same view later without having to reapply all the changes.

- **Group By:** Offers options to group the data by specific columns, which can help in summarizing and visualizing information.

- **Filtering and Reset:** Filtering enables users to apply filters to the data to focus on specific records or values that match certain criteria, while Reset allows users to reset any applied filters, sorting, or other customizations and revert to the default view.

In summary, the purpose of the Actions Menu is to provide users with a convenient way to interact with and manipulate the data presented in the Interactive Report and the Interactive Grid according to their needs.

CHARTS & CALENDAR

6

In Oracle APEX, a chart refers to a graphical representation of data that helps visualize and analyze information in a more accessible and intuitive way. APEX provides built-in functionality to create various types of charts within web applications without requiring extensive coding or complex configurations. These charts can be used to display trends, comparisons, distributions, and other insights from the underlying data.

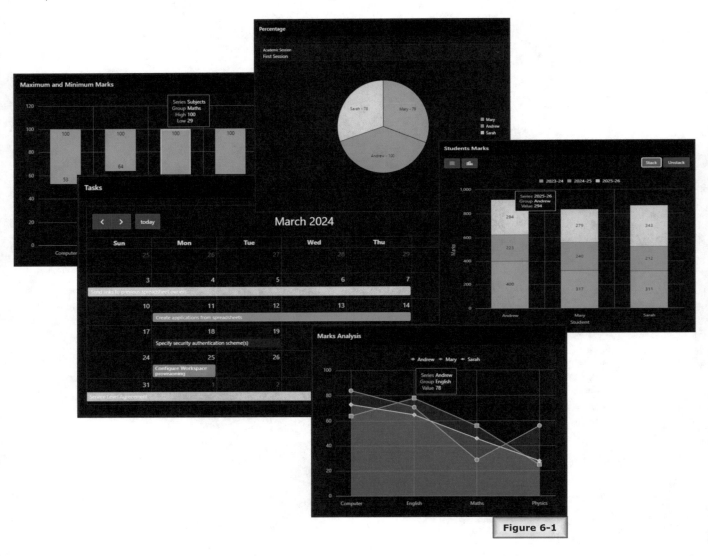

Figure 6-1

In Oracle APEX, you have the flexibility to create charts either as a region within a page or as an entire page dedicated to displaying a chart. The choice depends on your application's layout and design requirements. When you create a chart as a region within a page, it's embedded within the content of the page along with other regions like forms, reports, and other components. This approach is useful when you want to integrate the chart into an existing page layout or display multiple components together. Creating a chart page involves designing an entire page dedicated solely to displaying the chart. This can be useful when the chart is the primary focus of the page or when you want to provide a dedicated URL for accessing the chart. This approach is ideal when you want to provide a link to a specific chart or when the chart's data visualization is central to the user's experience.

Here are some key features and concepts related to charts in Oracle APEX:

Chart Types

APEX offers a range of chart types including line charts, bar charts, pie charts, area charts, scatter plots, and more. Each type is suited for different data visualization needs.

Interactive Features

APEX charts can be made interactive, allowing users to interact with the chart to explore data further. For example, you can enable drilldown capabilities, where clicking on a chart element reveals more detailed information.

Data Source

Charts in APEX can be populated with data from various sources, such as Local Tables, SQL queries, Web Services, and RESTful Web Sources. You typically define the data source from which the chart will retrieve the necessary data.

Integration

Charts can be linked to page items in your APEX application. This means that changes in the chart can update other parts of the application, providing a seamless user experience.

Series/Categories

Charts consist of one or more series, which represent the data to be visualized, and categories, which are used to group data points. For example, in a bar chart, each series could represent a different category and its associated values.

Dynamic

APEX allows you to define dynamic actions that are triggered by events on the chart. These actions can include refreshing the chart data, updating page items, or executing SQL statements.

Attributes

You can customize the appearance and behavior of charts using attributes. These attributes include settings for labels, colors, legends, tooltips, and more.

Responsive Design

APEX charts are designed to be responsive, meaning they can adapt to different screen sizes and devices, providing a consistent experience across desktops, tablets, and smartphones.

To create a chart in Oracle APEX, you typically start by selecting the chart type and defining the data source. Then, you configure the series, categories, attributes, and any interactive features as needed. APEX provides a user-friendly interface for these configurations, making it relatively straightforward to create and customize charts within your application.

BAR CHART

A bar chart in Oracle APEX is a type of graphical representation that displays data using rectangular bars. Each bar corresponds to a specific category or group, and the length or height of the bar represents the value of the data associated with that category. Bar charts are commonly used to compare values across different categories or to show changes in values over time.

In this segment, you will create a stacked bar chart. A stacked bar chart is a type of bar chart used in data visualization that displays multiple datasets as a series of stacked bars. In a stacked bar chart, each bar is divided into segments, and each segment represents a subset of the data within a particular category. The segments within a bar are stacked on top of each other, creating a cumulative representation of the total value for each category. Stacked bar charts are particularly useful when you want to highlight the composition of data categories, such as breaking down sales revenue by product categories or comparing the distribution of expenses across different cost categories. They provide a comprehensive visual representation of both the overall values and the relative proportions of data subsets. Open the Home page (Page 1) of the application in page designer to execute the following steps.

1. **Right-click the** Body **node and select** Create Region. **Set the following properties for the new region. Immediately after switching the region's Type, a new node named Series along with a child node (New) is added under the region. The query below fetches summarized marks figures by academic sessions for each student.**

The dualChart value mentioned for the Static ID property will be used in some JavaScripts in subsequent steps for chart animation. The Static ID property for a region is a unique identifier assigned to a specific region on a page. This property allows you to refer to the region using a consistent and recognizable identifier, making it easier to target the region for various purposes, such as applying dynamic actions, custom JavaScript, or CSS styling.

PROPERTY	VALUE
Title	Students Marks
Type	Chart
Location (Source)	Local Database
Type (Source)	SQL Query

SQL Query	SELECT s.student_id, s.student_name,
	      sum (decode(rm.academic_session,'2023-24',rd.marks,null)) "2023-24",
	      sum (decode(rm.academic_session,'2024-25',rd.marks,null)) "2024-25",
	      sum (decode(rm.academic_session,'2025-26',rd.marks,null)) "2025-26"
	FROM students s, results_master rm, results_details rd
	WHERE s.student_id = rm.student_id and rm.result_id = rd.result_id
	GROUP BY s.student_id, s.student_name
	ORDER BY s.student_name

Column Span	6 (to occupy initial half of the screen)
Static ID	dualChart

Here is the explanation of the SQL SELECT statement used for the chart:

A. SELECT Clause:

- s.student_id: Selects the `student_id` column from the `students` table.
- s.student_name: Selects the `student_name` column from the `students` table.
- SUM(DECODE(...)) AS "Year": For each academic year ('2023-24', '2024-25', '2025-26'), this calculates the sum of the `marks` column from the `results_details` table. The `DECODE` function is used to conditionally sum the marks based on the academic session. The result of each `SUM(DECODE(...))` calculation is aliased with the respective year ('2023-24', '2024-25', '2025-26').

B. FROM Clause:

- The `FROM` clause specifies the tables involved in the query: `students`, `results_master`, and `results_details`.
- The tables are given aliases (`s`, `rm`, `rd`) to make the SQL statement more concise.

C. WHERE Clause:

- s.student_id = rm.student_id: Joins the `students` and `results_master` tables based on the `student_id` column.
- rm.result_id = rd.result_id: Joins the `results_master` and `results_details` tables based on the `result_id` column.

D. GROUP BY Clause:

- GROUP BY s.student_id, s.student_name: Groups the results based on unique combinations of `student_id` and `student_name`.

E. ORDER BY Clause:

- ORDER BY s.student_name: Orders the final result set in ascending order of `student_name`.

This query retrieves data from three related tables (`students`, `results_master`, and `results_details`) to calculate the sum of marks for each student across different academic years. The result is structured with each student's ID, name, and sums of marks for each year. This query is used to create the stacked bar chart to display students' marks for different academic sessions.

2. Click the Attributes tab of the Students Marks chart region and set properties as defined in the adjacent table. The Stack property specifies whether the data items are stacked. We defined Automatic animation setting for the chart, which applies the Oracle JET's default animation settings. It specifies whether animation is shown when data is changed on the chart. A data change can occur if the chart gets automatically refreshed. In the current scenario, the animation takes place when you click one of the four buttons: Horizontal, Vertical, Stack, or Unstack. These buttons will be created in subsequent steps. The Hide and Show Behavior is performed when you click a legend item. For example, deselecting a legend item will hide its associated data series on the chart. With the value set to Rescale for this property, the chart rescales as you select or de-select a legend. This is useful for series with largely varying values.

PROPERTY	VALUE
Type	Bar
Title	*Leave it blank*
Orientation	Vertical
Stack	Turn On
Maximum Width	800
Height	400
On Data Change (Animation)	Automatic
Show (Legend)	Turn On
Position (Legend)	Top
Hide and Show Behavior	Rescale

3. Click the New node (under Series) and set these properties. Each series you create for your chart appears in a unique color to represent academic session and displays marks for each session (using the Value property) that is derived from the SELECT statement specified in step 1. You set Source Location (on row 2) to Region Source, which specifies that the data of this series is to be extracted from the SQL query defined for the Students Marks region (defined in step 1). In the third Label attribute you select a column name that is used for defining the label of the x-axis on the chart, while the 2023-24 column selected for the Value property is used for defining the marks for this session on the chart. When you click a chart bar (representing 2023-24), you'll be drilled down to Page 4, using the values set for the Target property, to browse student's details.

PROPERTY	VALUE
Name	2023-24
Location (Source)	Region Source
Label (Column Mapping)	STUDENT_NAME
Value	2023-24
Type (Link)	Redirect to Page in this Application
Target	Type = Page in this application Page = 4 Name = P4_STUDENT_ID Value = &STUDENT_ID. Clear Cache = 4
Show (Label)	Turn On
Position (Label)	Center

4. Right-click the Series node and select Create Series from the context menu to add another series. Set the adjacent properties for the new series. Use the same values as defined for the Type and Target properties in Step 3 to transform this series into a link to access Page 4.

PROPERTY	VALUE
Name	2024-25
Location (Source)	Region Source
Label (Column Mapping)	STUDENT_NAME
Value	2024-25
Show (Label)	Turn On
Position (Label)	Center

5. Create an additional chart series for the last academic session and configure its properties. Additionally, create a custom link by replicating the configurations you set up in the previous steps to provide interactivity.

PROPERTY	VALUE
Name	2025-26
Location (Source)	Region Source
Label (Column Mapping)	STUDENT_NAME
Value	2025-26
Show (Label)	Turn On
Position (Label)	Center

6. Click the x-axis node (under Axes) and enter Students for the Title property. This x-axis title will appear at the bottom of the chart.

7. Click the y-axis node (under Axes) and enter Marks for the Title property. This title will appear to the left of the chart.

8. In this step, you will add two buttons to the Students Marks region. When clicked, these buttons will change the chart's orientation using the default animation. Right-click the Students Marks region and select Create Button from the context menu. A new node named Region Body will be added with a button labeled New. Set the adjacent properties for this button. The Action attribute set for the button says that this button is associated with a dynamic action (defined in the next step), which fires when the button is clicked.

PROPERTY	VALUE
Button Name	Horizontal
Label	Horizontal
Position	Previous
Button Template	Icon
Icon	fa-bars
Action	Defined by Dynamic Action

Right-click the Horizontal button and select Duplicate from the context menu. A duplicate of this button named Horizontal_1 will be created just under it. Set properties for this new button as mentioned in the adjacent table.

PROPERTY	VALUE
Button Name	Vertical
Label	Vertical
Position	Previous
Button Template	Icon
Icon	fa-bar-chart
Action	Defined by Dynamic Action

9. Now add two dynamic actions for the two buttons. Click the Dynamic Actions tab, right-click the Click node, and select Create Dynamic Action. Click the New node and set the adjacent properties. This dynamic action is named Horizontal Orientation. The next three properties specify that this dynamic action should trigger when the Horizontal button is clicked.

PROPERTY	VALUE	
Name	Horizontal Orientation	
Event	Click	
Selection Type	Button	
Button	Horizontal	

Click the Show node under the True node to set the adjacent properties. When the Horizontal button is clicked, the JavaScript code is fired. In this code, 'dualChart' is the static ID you set in step 1 for the Students Marks region. You control chart's orientation through the 'ojChart' class, which has two options (Horizontal and Vertical), where Vertical is the default option. In this step, you inform the Oracle APEX engine to display the chart horizontally when the Horizontal button is clicked. Note that the chart orientation only applies to bar, line, area, combo, and funnel charts.

PROPERTY	VALUE	
Action	Execute JavaScript Code	
Code	$("#dualChart_jet").ojChart({orientation: 'horizontal'});	
Selection Type	Region	
Region	Students Marks	
Event	Horizontal Orientation	
Fire on Initialization	Turn Off	

10. Right-click the Click node and select Create Dynamic Action to add one more dynamic action for vertical orientation. Click the New node and set the adjacent properties.

PROPERTY	VALUE	
Name	Vertical Orientation	
Event	Click	
Selection Type	Button	
Button	Vertical	

Click the Show node under the True node and set these properties.

PROPERTY	VALUE	
Action	Execute JavaScript Code	
Code	$("#dualChart_jet").ojChart({orientation: 'vertical'});	
Selection Type	Region	
Region	Students Marks	
Event	Vertical Orientation	
Fire on Initialization	Turn Off	

11. Switch back to the Rendering tab. Add two more buttons under the previous two buttons. These buttons will be used to render the series data as stacked or unstacked. Set these properties for the two buttons.

PROPERTY	VALUE
Button Name	Stack
Label	Stack
Position	Next
Button Template	Text
Action	Defined by Dynamic Action

PROPERTY	VALUE
Button Name	Unstack
Label	Unstack
Position	Next
Button Template	Text
Action	Defined by Dynamic Action

12. Create a dynamic action to stack the chart when the Stack button is clicked. Set properties for the 'New' node as defined in the adjacent table.

PROPERTY	VALUE
Name	Stack Chart
Event	Click
Selection Type	Button
Button	Stack

Set properties for the Stack Chart dynamic event's Show node.

PROPERTY	VALUE
Action	Execute JavaScript Code
Code	$("#dualChart_jet").ojChart({stack: 'on'});
Selection Type	Region
Region	Students Marks
Event	Stack Chart
Fire on Initialization	Turn Off

Create another dynamic action to unstack the chart when the Unstack button is clicked. Set properties for the 'New' node as defined in the adjacent table.

PROPERTY	VALUE
Name	Unstack Chart
Event	Click
Selection Type	Button
Button	Unstack

The Unstack Chart dynamic event's Show node properties.

PROPERTY	VALUE
Action	Execute JavaScript Code
Code	$("#dualChart_jet").ojChart({stack: 'off'});
Selection Type	Region
Region	Students Marks
Event	Unstack Chart
Fire on Initialization	Turn Off

Save your progress. Launch the application and navigate to the Home section in the application's navigation menu. The chart, as illustrated in figure 6-2, will appear on the Home page. Hover your cursor over the chart bars and various sections within a bar. This action will reveal a tooltip displaying information about the session, student's name, and marks attained by the individual student. Experiment with the 'Vertical' and 'Horizontal' buttons to toggle the chart's orientation. Similarly, explore the 'Stack' and 'Unstack' buttons to observe the corresponding animated effects.

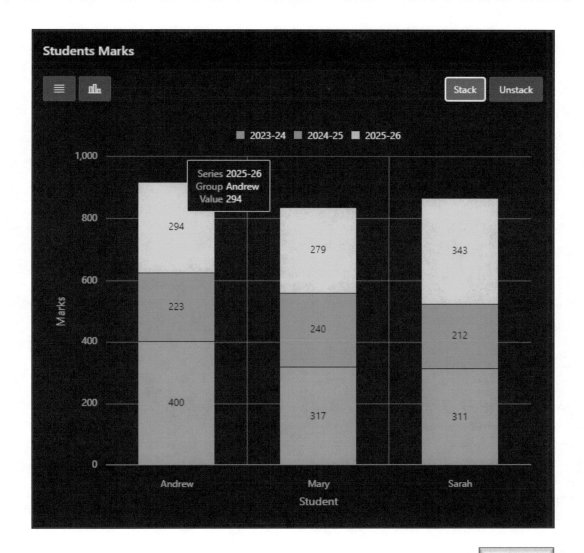

Figure 6-2

A pie chart is a type of data visualization that represents data in a circular graph. A pie chart displays data as slices of a pie, with each slice representing a portion of the whole. The size of each slice is proportional to the value it represents relative to the total value of the data set.

Pie charts are commonly used to display categorical data or to show the distribution of a single series of data points. Each slice of the pie corresponds to a category or data point, and the overall pie represents the total data set. The angles of the slices are determined by the relative values of the data points they represent. Pie charts are useful when you want to show the proportion of different categories within a whole. However, keep in mind that they can become less effective when there are too many categories or when the slices are very small and difficult to distinguish. In this section, you'll create a pie chart to depict students' percentages. Each student's portion will be illustrated as a slice within the circular graph, the size of which mirrors their percentage in the whole. This chart offers a quick visual grasp of academic achievement disparities among students.

1. Right-click the Body node and select Create Region. Set the following properties for the new region. The "Page Item(s) to Submit" property is used to specify which page items' values should be included when a page is submitted to the server. In this scenario, we will submit the value from the 'P1_ACADEMIC_SESSION' page item, which is a Select List. This item will be created and explained in a subsequent step. By deactivating the 'Start New Row' property, the resulting pie chart will be positioned alongside the stacked bar chart that was created in the previous exercise.

PROPERTY	VALUE	
Title	Percentage	
Type	Chart	
Location (Source)	Local Database	
Type (Source)	SQL Query	
SQL Query	SELECT st.student_name, rm.academic_session, sum(rd.marks) * 100/400 Percentage FROM students st, results_master rm, results_details rd WHERE st.student_id=rm.student_id and rm.result_id=rd.result_id and rm.academic_session=:P1_ACADEMIC_SESSION GROUP BY st.student_name, rm.academic_session	
Page Item(s) to Submit	P1_ACADEMIC_SESSION	
Start New Row	Turn Off	

Let's break down the given SQL SELECT statement step by step:

A. **SELECT Clause:**

- st.student_name: Selects the `student_name` column from the `students` table.
- rm.academic_session: Selects the `academic_session` column from the `results_master` table.
- SUM(rd.marks) * 100 / 400 AS Percentage: Calculates the percentage for each student using the `SUM` function to sum up the `marks` column from the `results_details` table, then multiplying it by `100` and dividing by `400` (assuming maximum marks of 400). The expression column is then aliased as `Percentage`.

B. **FROM Clause:**

- The `FROM` clause specifies the tables involved in the query: `students`, `results_master`, and `results_details`.
- The tables are given aliases (`st`, `rm`, `rd`) to make the SQL statement more concise.

C. **WHERE Clause:**

- st.student_id = rm.student_id: Joins the `students` and `results_master` tables based on the `student_id` column.
- rm.result_id = rd.result_id: Joins the `results_master` and `results_details` tables based on the `result_id` column.
- rm.academic_session = :P1_ACADEMIC_SESSION: Filters the results to include only rows where the academic_session` in the `results_master` table matches the value of the bind variable `:P1_ACADEMIC_SESSION`. This variable represents an item on the page. In this case, it is a Select List on the Home page carrying a list of academic sessions.

D. **GROUP BY Clause:**

- GROUP BY st.student_name, rm.academic_session: Groups the results based on the unique combinations of `student_name` and `academic_session`.

In summary, this query retrieves data from three related tables (`students`, `results_master`, and `results_details`) to calculate the percentage achieved by each student in a given academic session. The results are grouped by student name and academic session. This query is used to generate data for the pie chart that visualizes students' percentages in a specific academic session.

2. Click the Attributes tab of the Percentage chart region and set properties as defined in the adjacent table.

PROPERTY	VALUE
Type	Pie
Title	*Leave it blank*
Maximum Width	800
Height	384

3. Click the New node (under Series) and set properties as defined in the adjacent table. The 'Region Source' value selected in the 'Location' property specifies that the data for this pie chart is to be derived from the SQL SELECT statement defined for the 'Percentage' region. Each student's name will be presented as chart labels, and their corresponding percentages will be displayed as values. In the 'Display As' property, you determine how the labels should appear on the slices of the pie chart. By choosing the 'Label - Value' option, the labels will exhibit both the label and value information in the format: label - value. For instance, 'Andrew - 100'.

PROPERTY	VALUE
Name	Percentages
Location (Source)	Region Source
Label	STUDENT_NAME
Value	PERCENTAGE
Show (Label)	Turn On
Display As	Label - Value

4. Right-click the Percentage region, and select Create Page Item from the context menu. Set properties for the new page item as listed in the adjacent table. This is a 'Select List' page item that is linked to the 'ACADEMIC SESSIONS' LOV (List of Values). During runtime, this list will be displayed above the pie chart. When you choose an academic session from the list, the page is submitted and the chosen value is sent to the SQL query. Subsequently, the pie chart is dynamically updated to present the percentage distribution of students within the selected academic session.

PROPERTY	VALUE
Name	P1_ACADEMIC_SESSION
Type	Select List
Label	Academic Session
Page Action on Selection	Submit Page
Region	Percentage
Position	Region Body
Type (List of Values)	Shared Components
List of Values	ACADEMIC SESSIONS

Save your progress. Launch the Home page. The Pie chart resembling the one illustrated below will appear next to the stacked bar chart. The 'Label – Value' set for the 'Display As' property in step 3 displays the students' names and their percentages on the Pie chart slices. A pie chart is a circular chart that is divided into slices, each representing a proportion of a whole. Each slice's size is determined by the data it represents in relation to the total data set. The entire circle represents 100% of the data. Select any session from the Academic Session Select List. When you select a session, the Pie chart region gets refreshed and displays students' names and their percentages in different slices with different colors. Hover your cursor over the chart slices to see a tooltip displaying student's name and percentage. Try out the three legends provided on the right-hand side by enabling and disabling them. Enabling or disabling a legend in a pie chart in Oracle APEX has a visual impact on how the chart is displayed to users. When you disable a legend the corresponding slice on the Pie chart hides and the chart is rescaled to show the enabled categories only. On the other hand, enabling a legend reinstates the slice with the same rescale functionality.

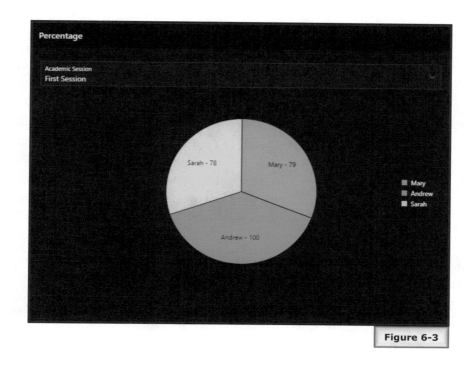

Figure 6-3

123

A range chart is a graphical representation used to display sets of data points, each of which is defined by two or more values for the same category. It emphasizes the range or difference between the highest and lowest values within each data point. Range charts are particularly useful when you need to visualize and compare the variability or spread of data across categories or time intervals. They are commonly used in statistics, quality control, finance, and various other fields to assess and display the extent of variation within a dataset.

Execute the following steps to create a Range chart to display maximum and minimum marks secured in each subject.

1. Once again, right-click the Body node and select Create Region. Set the following properties for the new region.

The query used for this chart retrieves a list of subjects along with their corresponding minimum and maximum marks from the results_details table, with one row per subject. This is useful for analyzing and comparing the performance of students in each subject, showing both the lowest and highest marks achieved in each subject.

PROPERTY	VALUE
Title	Maximum and Minimum Marks
Type	Chart
Location (Source)	Local Database
Type (Source)	SQL Query
SQL Query	SELECT subject, min(marks), max(marks) FROM results_details GROUP BY subject ORDER BY subject
Start New Row	Turn On
Column Span	6

2. Click the Attributes tab of this chart region and set properties as defined in the adjacent table.

PROPERTY	VALUE
Type	Range
Title	*Leave it blank*
Maximum Width	800
Height	400

3. Click the New node (under Series) and set properties as defined in the adjacent table.

PROPERTY	VALUE
Name	Subjects
Location (Source)	Region Source
Label	SUBJECT
Low	MIN(MARKS)
High	MAX(MARKS)
Show (Label)	Turn On

Save and Run the page. The Range chart resembling the one illustrated below will appear under the Stacked Bar chart. The chart reveals the highest and lowest marks for each subject.

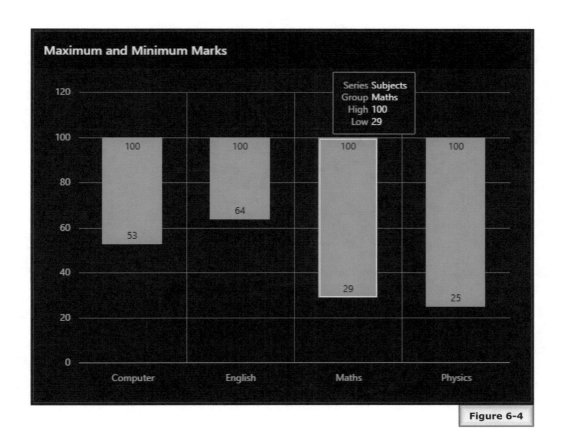

Figure 6-4

A line with area chart is a type of data visualization that combines elements of both a line chart and an area chart. It is used to represent data in a way that shows the trend of a variable over time or across categories, while also indicating the extent or magnitude of the values.

Follow these steps to create a Line with Area chart that displays students' marks obtained in various subjects during a specific academic session.

1. Right-click the Body node and select Create Region. Set the following properties for the new region.

The SQL query used for this chart combines data from three tables (students, results_master, and results_details) to fetch the marks earned by students in various subjects during a specified academic session. It links student and result information, filters by the academic session, and orders the results by student name. Essentially, the chart reveals students' performance in different subjects for a given academic term.

PROPERTY	VALUE
Title	Marks Analysis
Type	Chart
Location (Source)	Local Database
Type (Source)	SQL Query
SQL Query	SELECT s.student_name student, rd.subject subject, rd.marks marks FROM students s, results_master rm, results_details rd WHERE s.student_id = rm.student_id AND rm.result_id = rd.result_id AND rm.academic_session = :P1_ACADEMIC_SESSION ORDER BY s.student_name
Start New Row	Turn Off

2. Click the Attributes tab of this chart region and set properties as defined in the adjacent table.

PROPERTY	VALUE
Type	Line with Area
Title	*Leave it blank*
Maximum Width	800
Height	400
Show (Legend)	Turn On
Position	Top
Hide and Show Behavior	Rescale

3. Click the New node (under Series) and set properties as defined in the adjacent table. The last property will show markers in different shapes (square, circles, diamond and more). In data visualization and charting, markers are symbols or shapes used to represent individual data points on a chart. These markers can vary in shape, size, and color, and they are often placed at data coordinates to make the data points more visible and distinguishable.

PROPERTY	VALUE
Name	Marks Analysis
Location (Source)	Region Source
Series Name	STUDENT
Label	SUBJECT
Value	MARKS
Show (Marker)	Yes

Save and Run the page. Select an Academic Session from the Select List provided under the Percentage chart. The Line with Area chart region will be refreshed to show a chart resembling the one illustrated below. A line with area chart combines the benefits of both line charts (showing trends) and area charts (showing magnitude) to provide a comprehensive view of data. It is a useful visualization tool for conveying information about how a variable changes over time or across categories while highlighting its overall scale or volume.

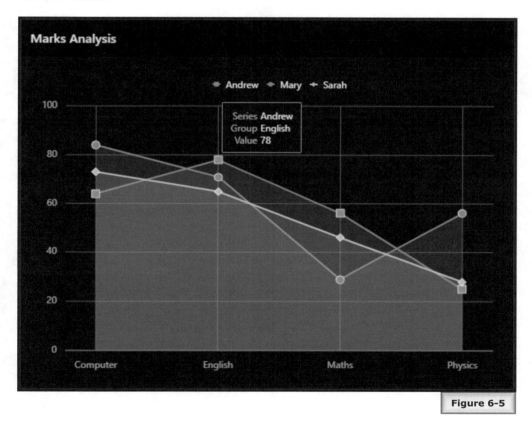

Figure 6-5

In Oracle APEX, the Calendar Page is a feature that allows you to display and interact with calendar data within your web applications. You can use it to create event calendars, appointment schedulers, or any other application that requires a visual representation of time-based data.

In addition to creating the Calendar page, you will utilize the SQL Commands interface, which is designed for interacting with your database. This interface allows you to retrieve data, update records, and perform various database operations. You will also learn how to use the Data Workshop to load data from an Excel file into a database table. Follow the steps below to create the calendar page.

1. Create a table named TASKS using the CREATE TABLE SQL statement, which is provided in the book code. Open SQL Workshop | SQL Commands (A). Copy and then paste the CREATE TABLE statement from the script file (Create-Table.txt) into the command area (B), and then click the Run button (C), as illustrated in the adjacent screen shot. A confirmation message "Table Created" will be displayed under the Results tab.

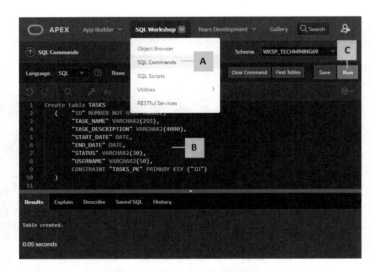

2. Now upload data from an Excel file into the TASKS table using the Data Workshop utility. Click SQL Workshop | Utilities | Data Workshop (D). On the Data Workshop page, click the Load Data option (E).

3. Then, on the Load Data page, select the Upload a File tab (F), and click the Choose File button (G). In the Open dialog box, select TASKS.XLSX file from BookCode\Chapter6 folder, and click Open.

4. On the Load Data screen, click the Existing Table option (H), select the TASKS table (I), and click the Load Data button (J). The Excel file columns will be mapped to the TASKS database table as illustrated in the Preview pane.

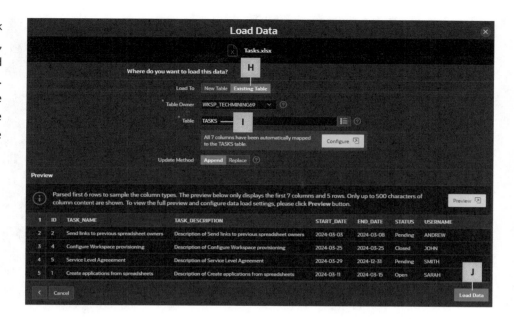

5. If everything goes well, the next screen appears with the message "Data in table TASKS appended with 5 new rows!". Click the View Table button to view the table in the Object Browser.

6. In the Object Browser, click the Data tab to view the uploaded data.

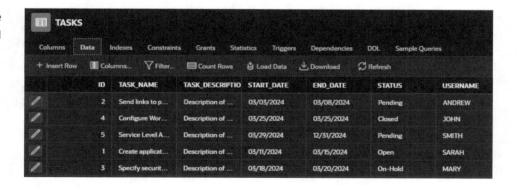

7. Now create the Calendar page. On the application home page, click the Create Page button and then select the Calendar option on the first wizard screen.

8. On the next wizard screen, fill in the Page Definition, Data Source, and Navigation information as illustrated here. Click Next to proceed.

The SQL query retrieves data from the TASKS table and calculates a derived column called CSS_CLASS based on the STATUS column's values. This derived column is used to determine how events on the calendar should be visually styled based on the status of the events. The key part of the query is the CASE statement, which is used to create the derived CSS_CLASS column. This column determines the CSS class that should be applied to each event when displayed on the calendar based on the value of the status column.

- When the status is 'Open,' it assigns the CSS class 'apex-cal-green' to the css_class column to show all such entries in green color.

- When the status is 'Pending,' it designates the 'apex-cal-yellow' CSS class to the 'css_class' column, resulting in all associated entries being displayed in yellow.

- When the status is marked as 'Closed,' it designates the 'apex-cal-red' CSS class for the 'css_class' column, causing all related entries to be presented in the color red.

- When the status is 'On-Hold,' it applies the 'apex-cal-black' CSS class to the 'css_class' column, resulting in all corresponding entries being displayed in black.

9. On the final wizard screen, configure column values as shown in the adjacent figure. When you select the END_DATE column, it will display the duration of events. If you wish to also show the time portion of the date, choose 'Yes' for 'Show Time.' The Week and Day views will only be visible when 'Show Time' is set to 'Yes.' If the start date or end date columns do not include time components, they will be displayed as 12:00 am. Click the Create Page button.

10. After creating the page, navigate to the Tasks region. In the Properties pane, switch to the Attributes tab. To display the name of the user assigned to each task, enter Assigned to &USERNAME. in the Supplemental Information property. At runtime, when you hover your mouse pointer over a task, the name of the user assigned to the task will be displayed in a tooltip.

Scroll down to locate the CSS Class property and select the CSS_CLASS column for this property. This will allow you to apply different styles and colors to tasks based on their status, as depicted in the screenshot below.

Once you've made these changes, save the page and run it. Then, using the arrow keys provided on the left-hand side, switch to March 2024. You should see the visual representation of the tasks in a calendar with the applied styling, similar to the following illustration.

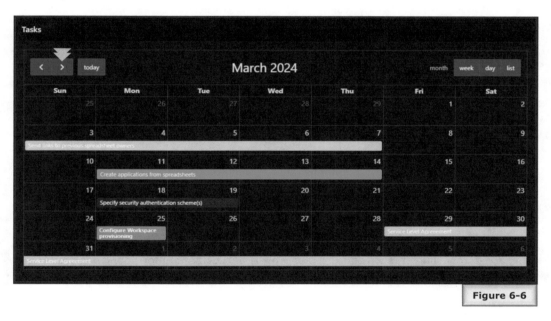

Figure 6-6

WHAT YOU LEARNED

In this chapter, we delved into the various ways of data visualization using Oracle APEX. We explored a range of chart types and other visual elements to effectively represent data within your applications. Here's a summary of the topics covered:

- Using Chart in Oracle APEX for Data Visualization: We began by understanding the importance of data visualization in Oracle APEX applications and how charts can be used to convey information visually.

- Bar Chart: We learned how to create Bar Charts in Oracle APEX, which are effective for comparing data across different categories or groups.

- Pie Chart: We explored Pie Charts, a great choice for displaying data as parts of a whole, such as percentages or proportions.

- Range Chart: Range Charts were discussed as a way to visualize data within a specific range, ideal for displaying data with upper and lower bounds.

- Line With Area Chart: We delved into Line with Area Charts, which combine line charts for displaying trends over time with filled areas to highlight data areas.

- Calendar: We looked at how to implement and customize Calendar pages in Oracle APEX, enabling users to view and interact with time-based data.

- SQL Commands: We explored the use of SQL commands interface in Oracle APEX, which is used to interact with databases, retrieve data, update records, and perform various database operations. SQL commands are essential for powering the data behind our visualizations.

- Data Workshop: We learned about the Data Workshop utility in Oracle APEX, which facilitates the process of importing data from external sources, such as Excel files. This is a valuable tool for populating your application's database with data from other sources.

By covering these topics, you now have a comprehensive understanding of data visualization, chart types, and data management tools available in Oracle APEX. This knowledge will enable you to create engaging and informative applications that effectively convey data insights to your users.

7

SEARCHING & FILTERING DATA

Oracle APEX provides various options for searching and filtering data within your web applications. These options allow users to query and narrow down datasets based on their specific criteria. Here are some of the common ways to search and filter data in Oracle APEX:

Interactive Reports

Interactive Reports are a powerful feature in Oracle APEX that allows users to filter and search data interactively. Users can easily customize the report layout, sort columns, and apply filters to view only the data they need.

Interactive Grid

Interactive Grids in Oracle APEX offer extensive filtering options. Users can filter data by entering values in filter cells, selecting filter conditions, and using dynamic actions to create custom filters.

Faceted Search

Faceted Search is a feature that enables users to drill down into data using a set of facets (attributes or dimensions). This approach is useful for refining search results in structured data.

Smart Filters

The Smart Filters region simplifies searching by offering multiple filters to refine results in real-time, creating a streamlined user experience.

Search Bar

You can add a search bar to your application that allows users to enter search terms to filter records based on specific columns or attributes.

Master Detail

Creating master-detail relationships between regions or reports allows users to filter data in one region based on the selection in another. This is particularly useful for displaying related data.

Dynamic Actions

You can use dynamic actions to define custom filtering logic. For example, you can create a dynamic action that filters a report based on user input in a text field.

Save Reports

Oracle APEX allows users to save customized reports with their preferred filter settings. These saved reports can be shared with others or set as default views.

SQL Queries

Advanced users can leverage custom SQL queries to filter data using specific criteria. This approach provides flexibility but may require SQL expertise.

Drilldown Charts

Charts in Oracle APEX can provide drilldown capabilities, allowing users to click on chart elements to filter data in related reports or charts.

These options provide a range of choices for developers and users to search and filter data in Oracle APEX applications, making it a versatile platform for building data-driven web applications. The choice of which option to use depends on the specific requirements and user experience you want to create for your application.

BASIC SEARCH

The Interactive Report provides a search bar at the top-right corner. Users can enter keywords in this search bar to perform a basic text-based search across all columns of the report.

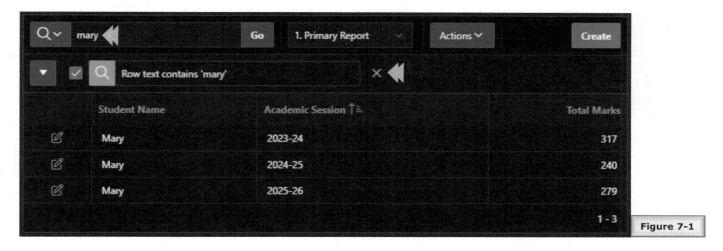

Figure 7-1

1. Location and Functionality:
   ▪ The basic search feature is typically located at the top-right corner of the Interactive Report interface.
   ▪ It serves as a text input field where users can enter keywords or search terms.

2. Search Across All Columns:
   ▪ When users enter a search term and press Enter, the basic search feature performs a search across all visible columns in the report. It scans the data in these columns to find any occurrences of the entered search term.
   ▪ Using the dropdown list provided on the left side, you can search data in a specific column.

3. Text-Based Search:
   ▪ The basic search is primarily text-based. Users can input words or phrases they are looking for in the report's data.
   ▪ For example, if an Interactive Report contains data about employees, a user might enter "John" in the search bar to find all records related to employees named John.

4. Partial Match:
   ▪ The basic search usually performs a partial match by default, meaning it finds rows containing the search term anywhere within the text in the columns.

5. Clearing the Search:
   ▪ Users can typically clear the filter by using the "X" icon provided by the interface.
   ▪ Clearing the search restores the report to its original state, displaying all data rows.

BASIC FILTER

In Oracle APEX Interactive Reports, the "Filter" option in the "Actions" menu allows users to apply filters to specific columns. Here's how users can use this feature to search data in a specific column:

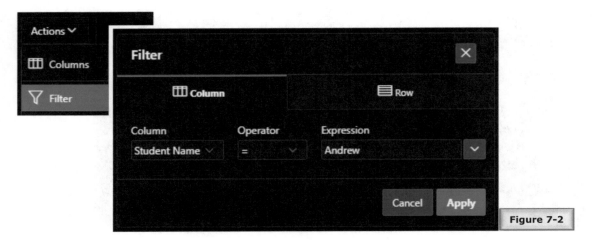

Figure 7-2

1. Accessing the "Filter" Option:
   - Users begin by opening the Interactive Report that they want to filter.
   - They should select the Filter option from the Actions menu. This action opens a filter dialog.

2. Applying the Filter:
Users can specify their search criteria within the filter dialog.
   - Select a column name – for example, `Student Name`.
   - Select an operator from the Operator list – for example `=`.
   - Type an expression – for example `Andrew`.

3. Performing the Search:
   - After entering their search criteria, users can activate the filter by clicking the "Apply" button within the dialog. This action applies the filter to the specific column.

4. Viewing Filtered Results:
   - Once the filter is applied, the Interactive Report updates to display only the rows that meet the search criteria within the selected column. Users will see a subset of data that matches their filter conditions for that specific column.

5. Clearing or Resetting Filters:
   - Users can clear or reset column filters to return the report to its original state, displaying all data rows. The "X" icon is typically the option to clear the filter conditions.

FACETED SEARCH

The Faceted Search feature in Oracle APEX allows users to refine and filter data within an application by using a set of facets, which are attributes or dimensions of the data. It provides a powerful and interactive way to explore large datasets, enabling users to narrow down their search results based on multiple criteria simultaneously.

Figure 7-3

Here are the key aspects and benefits of the Faceted Search feature in Oracle APEX:

- Facets: Facets represent attributes or columns in your data. They could be things like product categories, dates, locations, or any other relevant data attributes. Users can select facets to filter data based on these attributes.

- Interactive Interface: Faceted Search provides an interactive interface that typically appears as a panel alongside a report or a grid. Users can select or deselect facets to view available values and apply filters with just a few clicks.

- Multiple Selections: Users can select multiple values within a facet, allowing for complex filtering combinations. For example, they can filter products by selecting multiple categories and brands.

- Real-Time Updates: As users select facets and values, the report or grid dynamically updates in real-time to display only the data that matches the selected criteria. This provides instant feedback and makes the process of narrowing down data very intuitive.

- Count of Matches: Faceted Search typically shows the count of matching records for each facet value. Users can see how many records match each criterion, aiding in decision-making.

- Adaptive and Responsive: Faceted Search is often adaptive and responsive, meaning it can adapt to different screen sizes and orientations, making it suitable for various devices.

Execute the following steps to create a Faceted Search page.

1. On the application home page, click the Create Page button and then select the Faceted Search option on the first wizard screen.

2. On the next wizard screen, fill in the page definition as illustrated here. The page will fetch data from the STUDENTS table, and its entry will appear under the Report menu. Click Next to proceed.

3. On the next wizard screen, select the Cards option, and then click the Refresh button. The Gender and Class columns from the table will be selected as facets for the page. The "Display as" option refers to how facet elements are presented to users in the facet region. When you choose "Display as: Cards" for a facet in Faceted Search, it presents the facet values as a series of cards, as illustrated above in figure 7-3. Each facet value is typically represented as a card that includes an image or icon (if available) along with other column values. The card format is more visually appealing and is commonly used when the facets have associated images or when a more modern and visual representation is preferred. On the other hand, when you choose "Display As: Report" for a facet, it presents the facet values in a tabular format. Click Next to proceed.

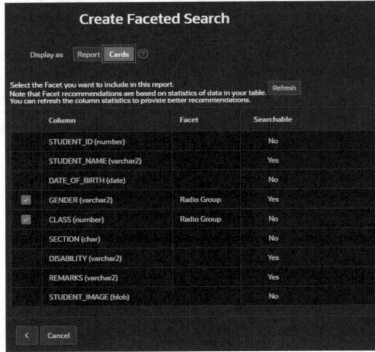

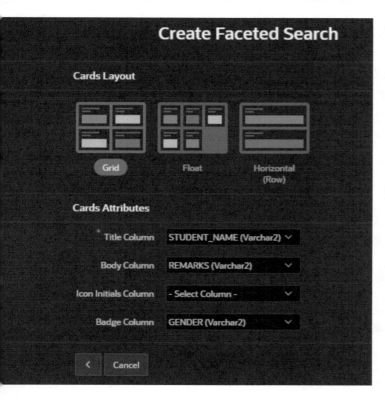

Create Faceted Search

Cards Layout

Grid   Float   Horizontal (Row)

Cards Attributes

* Title Column	STUDENT_NAME (Varchar2) ⌄
Body Column	REMARKS (Varchar2) ⌄
Icon Initials Column	- Select Column - ⌄
Badge Column	GENDER (Varchar2) ⌄

< | Cancel

4. On the final wizard screen, select the Grid option for the Cards Layout. Select values in the Cards Attributes section as illustrated in the adjacent figure. The Grid layout is a way to display the search results in a grid format. This layout is similar to a traditional table layout, but the cards are arranged in a grid, with multiple cards per row. The Float layout displays the search results in a floating format. This layout is similar to a grid layout, but the cards are not arranged in a fixed grid. Instead, they are floated around the page, and the user can scroll to see more cards. The Horizontal (Row) layout displays the search results in a horizontal row. This layout is similar to a list layout, but the cards are arranged horizontally, instead of vertically. The "Title Column" is the column in your facet source that provides the primary text or title displayed on the facet value cards. This text is typically the most important and descriptive information about the facet value. The "Body Column" is the column that supplies additional content or details related to the facet value. It is often displayed as a secondary description. The "Badge Column" is used to display supplementary information in a small, badge-like element on the facet value card. Click the Create Page button to complete the process.

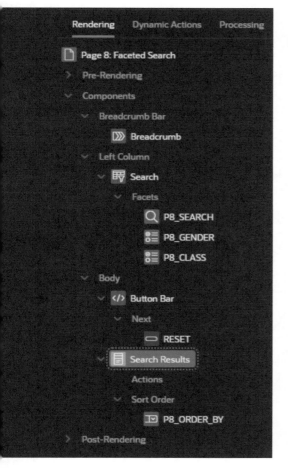

Rendering   Dynamic Actions   Processing

📄 Page 8: Faceted Search
> Pre-Rendering
∨ Components
  ∨ Breadcrumb Bar
      ⟫⟫ Breadcrumb
  ∨ Left Column
    ∨ 🔢 Search
      ∨ Facets
          🔍 P8_SEARCH
          ≔ P8_GENDER
          ≔ P8_CLASS
  ∨ Body
    ∨ </> Button Bar
      ∨ Next
          ⊝ RESET
    ∨ 📄 Search Results
        Actions
      ∨ Sort Order
          P8_ORDER_BY
> Post-Rendering

Prior to executing this page, let's examine the wizard's contributions.

A Search Region: The Search region contains a search box and two facets – Gender and Class. The search box allows you to search for any student information. For example, you can enter a student's name or any keyword stored in the 'Remarks' column. The 'Gender' facet is displayed as a Radio Group, presenting multiple values as radio group options, allowing the end user to select a single value, either 'Female' or 'Male.' When you choose any of these options, the cards on the right side are updated to display students of the selected gender. The 'Class' facet functions similarly to the 'Gender' facet, offering two options: 'Class 7' and 'Class 8.' Upon selecting one of these options, a filter is applied and displayed above the 'Order By' select list. To remove the filter, click the 'x' symbol next to it or select 'Clear' from the facets pane. Other available facet types include Checkbox Group, Input Field, Range, Search, and Select List.

B Reset Button: By using this button, you can remove all filters applied to the page and restore the information to its default state.

C Search Result Region: This is the region that appears on the right side and displays students' information in cards. The "Order by" property in a faceted page Card region controls the order by select list that is displayed under the region.

D Sort Order: This select list appears above the cards report, allowing you to sort students' information by name, gender, and remarks.

After creating the page, execute the steps below to display and style students' images:

1. Click the Search Results card region. On the Region tab in the property editor, scroll down to the Appearance section. Click the Template Options property. In the Template Options dialog box, select Style B for Style property.

2. In the property editor, click the Attributes tab to set the properties as shown in the adjacent table. The primary key will be used to get the student image. The last two properties set the image source.

PROPERTY	VALUE
Primary Key Column 1	STUDENT_ID
Icon Source	Image BLOB Colum
Image Column	STUDENT_IMAGE

Save the changes and run the page. Use the search box and the two facets to filter the data. Also use the Order By select list to sort the data.

You can go through a more detailed example of the Faceted Search feature with multiple facet types, including range, select list, and checkboxes on my YouTube channel https://www.youtube.com/@TechMining69.

Smart Filters is a search component and it is a simplified version of Faceted Search that is easier to use and has a smaller footprint. Smart Filters consists of a single search field and a list of suggestion chips. The suggestion chips are based on the data that is being searched and are updated as the user types in the search field. The user can click on a suggestion chip to filter the data by that value.

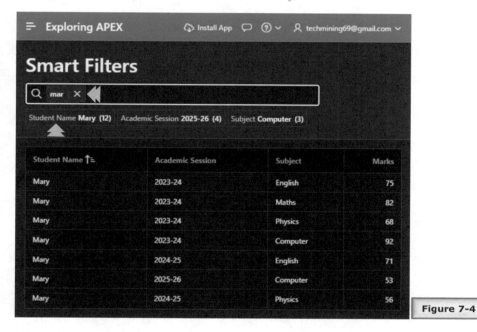

Figure 7-4

Smart Filters also has a number of features that make it more user-friendly than Faceted Search, such as:

- Autocomplete: The search field in Smart Filters supports autocomplete, which makes it easier for users to find the values they are looking for.
- Dynamic filtering: Smart Filters updates the suggestion chips as the user types in the search field. This allows users to quickly filter the data without having to leave the search field.
- Multi-value filtering: Smart Filters supports multi-value filtering, which allows users to filter the data by multiple values at the same time.
- Nested filtering: Smart Filters supports nested filtering, which allows users to create complex filters by combining multiple filters.

Here are some examples of how Smart Filters can be used:

- Searching for products in an e-commerce application: Users can use Smart Filters to search for products by name, price, category, and other criteria.
- Searching for employees in a human resources application: Users can use Smart Filters to search for employees by name, department, job title, and other criteria.
- Searching for customers in a CRM application: Users can use Smart Filters to search for customers by name, company name, industry, and other criteria.

Execute the following steps to create a Faceted Search page.

1. On the application home page, click the Create Page button and then select the Smart Filters option on the first wizard screen.

2. On the next wizard screen, fill in the page definition as illustrated here. The page will fetch data from the STUDENTS and RESULTS_DETAILS tables using a SQL query, which was used in Chapter 5. Click Next to proceed.

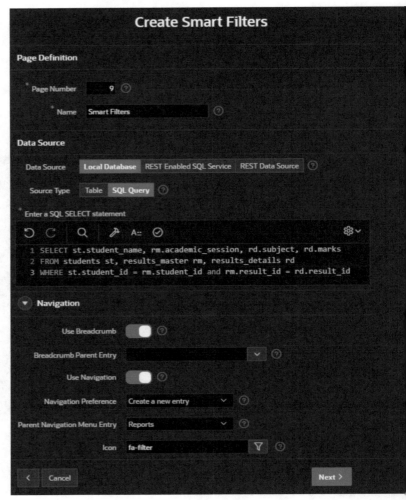

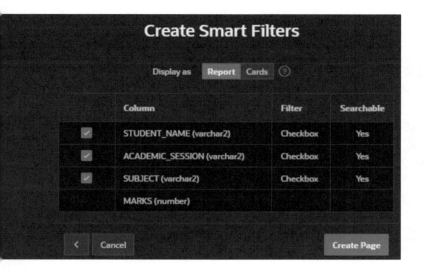

3. On the final wizard screen, select the default Report option for 'Display as', and accept all three suggested filters for the report. Click Create Page to complete the process.

Run the page. If you click on the chip label (Student Name), you'll see a list of other values for that filter. You can make multiple selections from this list, and the report data will update instantly.

The Smart Filters feature also searches across multiple columns. This means that when you enter a value in the search bar, Smart Filter looks for that value in all columns. For instance, if you type 'mar' in the search box and press Enter, you will see records that include 'Mary.' To clear the filter and restore the report to its original state, use the x icon.

WHAT YOU LEARNED

In this chapter, we explored various data search and filtering features in Oracle APEX, enhancing the user's ability to navigate and extract insights from their data. The key topics covered include Basic Search, Basic Filters, Faceted Search, and Smart Filters.

Basic Search (Interactive Report and Interactive Grid):
- Basic Search allows users to perform keyword-based searches within Interactive Reports and Interactive Grids.
- Users can enter search terms in a dedicated search bar to filter data rows that contain matching keywords.
- Basic Search provides a quick and text-based way to locate specific information within large datasets.

Basic Filters (using Actions menu):
- Basic Filters are used to narrow down data within Interactive Reports and Interactive Grids.
- Users can access the "Filter" option in the Actions menu for specific columns to define filtering criteria.
- Applying these filters allows for refined data analysis by selecting the criteria that meet specific requirements.

Faceted Search:
- Faceted Search is a powerful tool for data filtering and exploration.
- Users can filter data based on multiple facets, which represent attributes or dimensions of the data.
- Facets offer interactive options like Radio Group, Checkbox Group, Select List, and Range.
- This feature is ideal for navigating large datasets by allowing users to apply multiple filters simultaneously.

Smart Filters:
- Smart Filters enhance the search experience by searching for values across multiple columns.
- Users can input search terms in the search bar, and Smart Filters look for matches in all columns.
- The feature provides a convenient way to find information across diverse data fields and can be cleared using a cross icon.

These search and filtering capabilities empower users to interact with their data effectively, making data-driven decisions and obtaining valuable insights from their Oracle APEX applications. The combination of Basic Search, Basic Filters, Faceted Search, and Smart Filters offers a comprehensive toolkit for managing and exploring data with ease and precision.

8

EXTENDING

APPLICATIONS

Oracle APEX offers a wide range of features that can be used to enhance the productivity of web applications. By using these features, you can create applications that are faster, more reliable, easier to use, and easier to develop and maintain. Here are some features that you can use to make your applications more productive.

Progressive Web Applications

PWAs are web applications that can be installed on a user's device like a native mobile app. They can be used offline, and they can send push notifications. PWAs are a great way to improve the user experience of Oracle APEX applications, and they can also help to increase productivity by making it easier for users to access the applications and stay up-to-date on the latest information.

Push Notifications

Push notifications can be used to send messages to users' devices, even when the applications are not open. This can be useful for sending alerts about important events, such as new orders or incoming messages. Push notifications can help to improve productivity by keeping users informed and allowing them to take action quickly.

Maps

Oracle APEX includes a built-in map component that can be used to display maps on web pages. This can be useful for applications that need to display geographic data, such as customer locations or field service territories. Using maps can help to improve productivity by making it easier for users to visualize and understand data.

In addition to the features listed above, Oracle APEX also offers a number of other features that can be used to improve productivity, such as:

- Version control: Oracle APEX includes a built-in version control system that allows you to track changes to your applications and revert to previous versions if necessary.
- Code sharing: Oracle APEX allows you to share code between different applications. This can help to reduce the amount of code that you need to write and maintain.
- Debugging tools: Oracle APEX includes a number of debugging tools that can help you to identify and fix errors in your applications.
- Performance monitoring: Oracle APEX includes a performance monitoring tool that can help you to identify and optimize performance bottlenecks in your applications.

PROGRESSIVE WEB APPLICATION

A Progressive Web Application (PWA) is a type of web application that is designed to be fast, reliable, and engaging. PWAs are built using modern web technologies, such as service workers and the Web App Manifest, which allow them to provide features that are typically associated with native mobile apps, such as offline support, push notifications, and the ability to be installed on the user's home screen.

Oracle APEX provides native support for PWAs, making it easy to create PWAs using the same development tools and techniques that you would use to create any other type of APEX application. To create a PWA in APEX, simply enable the "Install Progressive Web App" feature when creating a new application (see Chapter 2), or by editing the attributes of an existing application.

Once you have enabled the "Install Progressive Web App" feature, you can configure various PWA attributes, such as the application name, description, icon, and theme color. You can also choose to enable or disable specific PWA features, such as offline support and push notifications.

Once you have configured the PWA attributes, you can deploy your application to a production environment. Once the application is deployed, users will be able to install it on their home screen and use it like any other native mobile app.

Here are some of the benefits of using PWAs in Oracle APEX:

- Improved performance: PWAs are typically faster than traditional web applications because they use service workers to cache static assets and serve them offline.
- Improved reliability: PWAs can continue to work even when the user is offline.
- Improved engagement: PWAs can provide features that are typically associated with native mobile apps, such as push notifications and the ability to be installed on the user's home screen.

Overall, PWAs offer a number of advantages over traditional web applications. If you are developing a web application that you want to be fast, reliable, and engaging, then you should consider using PWAs in Oracle APEX.

Here are some examples of how PWAs can be used in Oracle APEX:

- Employee portal: A PWA-based employee portal can give employees access to important company information and resources, even when they are offline.
- Customer relationship management (CRM) system: A PWA-based CRM system can give sales reps access to customer data and lead tracking tools, even when they are on the go.
- Field service management (FSM) system: A PWA-based FSM system can give field technicians access to work orders, customer information, and spare parts inventory, even when they are in remote locations.

These are just a few examples of how PWAs can be used in Oracle APEX. With their many advantages, PWAs are a great way to improve the user experience of your web applications.

You can enable the Progressive Web App (PWA) feature when creating a new application (refer to Chapter 2) or in an existing application as follows:

1. Go to Shared Components and click User Interface Attributes in the User Interface section.

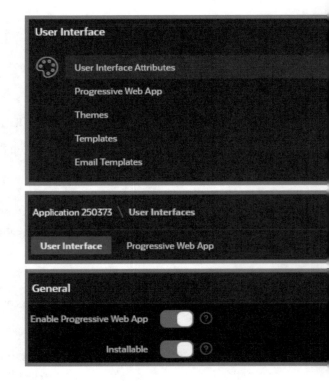

2. Then, click the Progressive Web App tab. Turn on the Enable Progressive Web App option. Also enable the Installable option that appears when you turn on the first option. Click the Apply Changes button.

When enabling the Progressive Web App (PWA) feature in Oracle APEX, you gain access to a range of options to enhance your application:

- Offline Support: The PWA can cache static assets for improved performance, even without an internet connection.

- Push Notifications: Send alerts about important events to users.

- Display Mode: Choose how much of the browser UI is visible when using the PWA, with options like Fullscreen, Standalone, Minimal UI, or Browser.

- Orientation: Control the allowed orientation (portrait, landscape, or any) of the PWA.

- Theme Color: Define the theme color used in the browser UI.

- Background Color: Customize the PWA's background color.

- Status Bar Style (for iOS): Select the style of the status bar on iOS devices.

- App Description: The app description explains what the application does. This is used to provide more information to users when they are prompted to install the application.

- Custom Manifest Properties: Specify custom properties in the PWA manifest for details like name, description, and icon.

Once you have turned on the PWA and installable options, users can install your application on their devices. To do this, users can visit your application in a web browser and tap on the "Install App" option in the navigation bar.

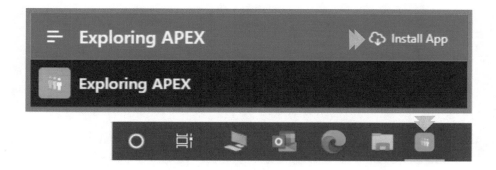

When a user installs your application, the following happens:

- The PWA manifest is installed on the user's device. This provides information about your application to the user's device.
- The service worker is installed on the user's device. This allows your application to run offline and send push notifications.
- A shortcut to your application is created on the user's home screen. This allows users to launch your application directly from their home screen.

Oracle APEX push notifications allow you to send real-time updates and alerts to your users' devices, even when they are not actively using your application. This can be a great way to keep users engaged and informed about important events, such as new messages, task assignments, or system outages.

APEX push notifications are supported on both desktop and mobile devices, and can be sent using a variety of methods, including:

- Native page process: This is the simplest way to send push notifications, and does not require any coding. To send a notification using a native page process, simply create a new page process and select the "Send Push Notification" action.
- Apex PWA API: The Apex PWA API provides more flexibility for sending push notifications, and allows you to customize the notification message and behavior. To use the Apex PWA API, you will need to create a custom page process that calls the apex_pwa.send_notification function.

To receive push notifications, users must first enable them in their application settings. Once enabled, users will receive a notification on their device whenever an event occurs that you have configured to trigger a notification.

Benefits of using Oracle APEX push notifications:

- Improved user engagement: Push notifications can help you to keep your users engaged with your application by providing them with real-time updates and alerts.
- Increased productivity: Push notifications can help users to be more productive by notifying them of important events, such as new task assignments or upcoming deadlines.
- Reduced support costs: Push notifications can help to reduce your support costs by providing users with timely information and preventing them from having to contact support for assistance.

Examples of use cases for Oracle APEX push notifications:

- Send a notification to a user when they receive a new message.
- Notify a user when a task is assigned to them.
- Alert a user when a system outage occurs.
- Send a reminder to a user about an upcoming deadline.
- Notify a user when a new product is released.

Overall, Oracle APEX push notifications are a powerful tool that can be used to improve the user experience, increase productivity, and reduce support costs.

You can enable the Push Notifications feature when creating a new application (refer to Chapter 2) or in an existing application. The Push Notifications feature can be enabled in an existing application from the same User Interface Attributes page from where you enable the PWA in the previous section. Here are the steps to enable this feature:

1. Go to Shared Components and click User Interface Attributes in the User Interface section.

2. Click the Progressive Web App tab. Make sure that Enable Progressive Web App and Installable options are enabled.

3. Scroll down a bit to the Push Notifications section and turn on the Enable Push Notifications switch. that appears when you turn on the first option. Click the Generate Credentials button.

4. Click the Apply Changes button.

Credentials in Push Notifications are used to authenticate with the push notification service provider (such as Google, Mozilla, or Apple). This ensures that only authorized applications can send push notifications to users. The Generate Credentials button is used to generate a new key pair credential for the application. This credential is used to authenticate with the push notification service provider and send push notifications to users.

When you enable Push Notifications in Oracle APEX, you will be prompted to either choose an existing key pair credential or generate a new one. If you do not have an existing credential, you should generate a new one.

To generate a new credential, simply click the Generate Credentials button. APEX will generate a new key pair credential and store it in the database. You can then use this credential to send push notifications to users. After clicking the button, its label changes to Regenerate Credentials.

The Contact Email in the Push Notifications section is used by the push notification service provider (such as Google, Mozilla, or Apple) to contact the application owner if needed. For example, the push notification service provider may contact the application owner if there is a problem with the push notification service, or if the application owner needs to provide additional information about their application.

5. Now create a new user who will receive the push notifications. Click the Administration icon and then click the Manage Users and Groups option. On the Manage Users and Groups page, click the Users tab. Click the Create User button. On the Create User page, enter a username (for example, John). Type the user's email address (for example, john@abcglobal.com). Scroll down to the Password section. Enter and confirm case sensitive user's password. Click the Create User button. The new user will be added to the users list.

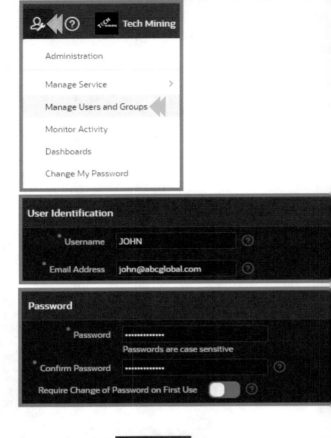

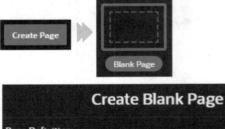

6. Create a new blank page. This page will provide some parameters to the 'send push notification' process. On the application home page, click the Create Page button and then select the Blank Page option on the first wizard screen. Fill in the page definition as illustrated here. The page will be invoked from the Administration menu. After providing the definitions, click the Create Page button.

   A blank page in Oracle APEX is a page that does not contain any pre-built components. This gives you complete control over the design and layout of the page, and allows you to implement any functionality that you require.

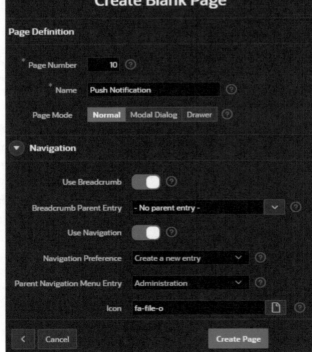

7. After creating the page, create a new region of static content type. This region will hold three text field page items for sending notifications. Right-click the Body node and select Create Region from the context menu. In the property editor, enter Push Notifications for region Title, and select Static Content for its Type.

A static content type region in Oracle APEX is a region that can be used to display any HTML content. This can be used to display simple text, images, tables, or even complex HTML layouts. We will create some text field page items under this region to send push notifications.

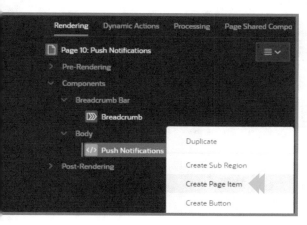

8. Now add three Text Field items to the static content region. Right-click the Push Notifications region, and select Create Page Item from the context menu. This action will add a new page item under the region. Set properties of this new page item as shown in the following figure.

In this first page item we will provide the user to whom we want to send the push notification.

A text field type page item in Oracle APEX is a page item that allows users to enter text. Text field type page items can be used to collect a variety of data, such as names, addresses, email addresses, and phone numbers. The name property is a unique identifier for the page item. The name property is used by Oracle APEX to reference the page item in code and expressions. The name property must be unique within the page. The label property is the text that is displayed to the user for the page item. The label property is used to describe the data that the user is expected to enter in the page item.

Page items in Oracle APEX are prefixed by default with the letter P and the page number. For example, a page item on page 1 would be prefixed with P1_. This prefixing convention is used to help ensure that page items are unique and to avoid conflicts with other page elements, such as regions and components. It is also best practice to include the page number in the page item prefix. This can make it easier to identify and debug page items when working with complex applications. Here are some examples of page item prefixes:
P1_FIRST_NAME, P2_LAST_NAME, P3_EMAIL_ADDRESS,
P4_PHONE_NUMBER, and P5_ADDRESS.

9. Add two more Text Field page items to the region, as shown in the adjacent table. In the second page item we will provide the notification title. And in this third page item we will enter the notification message.

PROPERTY	VALUE
Name	P10_TITLE
Type	Text Field
Label	Title

PROPERTY	VALUE
Name	P10_MESSAGE
Type	Text Field
Label	Message

10. Add a button to the page. Once this button is clicked, the notification will be dispatched to the selected user. Set the button properties as indicated in the table below the image.

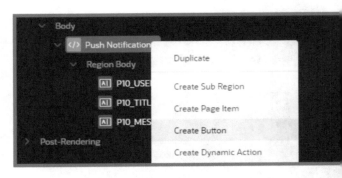

A button in Oracle APEX is a page component that allows users to perform an action, such as submitting a page, redirecting to another page, or calling a JavaScript function. Buttons can be displayed anywhere on a page and can be customized to have a variety of appearances.

The button name is a unique identifier for the button. The button name is used by Oracle APEX to reference the button in code and expressions. The button name must be unique within the page.

PROPERTY	VALUE
Button Name	SEND
Label	Send
Position (Layout)	Copy
Action (Behavior)	Submit Page

The label is the text that is displayed on the button. The label is used to describe the action that the button will perform when clicked.

The copy position property determines where the button will be displayed in the page layout. If the region has a title bar, the button will be placed on the right side of the title bar, next to the region's name.

The action property determines what action the button will perform when clicked. The action property can be set to one of the following values:

- Submit Page: The page will be submitted.
- Redirect to Page: The user will be redirected to the specified page.

In the current scenario, we selected the Submit Page action that will trigger a page process named Send Push Notification, which will be created next.

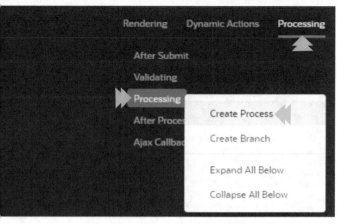

PROPERTY	VALUE
Name	Send Notification
Type	Send Push Notification
To	&P10_USER.
Title	&P10_TITLE.
Body	&P10_MESSAGE.
Success Message	Notification sent successfully to the user.
Error Message	Error encountered while sending the notification.
When Button Pressed	SEND

11. Next, create a new process to send notifications. In Page Designer, click the Processing tab. Right-click the Processing node, and select Create Process from the context menu. Set properties of this process as depicted in the table. We set the type of this process to Send Push Notification. The built-in Send Push Notification process is a process that can be used to send push notifications to users. This process is very versatile and can be used to implement a variety of functionality. We also used three substitution variables (&P10_USER., &P10_TITLE., and &P10_MESSAGE.) instead of hard-coding the user name, title, and the notification message. With this dynamic approach, the name you enter in the P10_USER page item will be used by this process to send the notification. We used the same approach for the notification title and message.

Substitution variables are used to dynamically insert values into SQL, PL/SQL, and other parts of your APEX application. To reference page or application items using substitution variables:

- Reference the page or application item in all capital letters.
- Precede the item name with an ampersand (&).
- Append a period (.) to the item name.

If the process runs successfully without generating any errors, then the text mentioned in the Success Message property will be displayed. If an unhandled exception is raised, then this error message will pop up. We associated this process with the SEND button, which means that the process will be executed only when the SEND button is pressed.

Save and run the page.

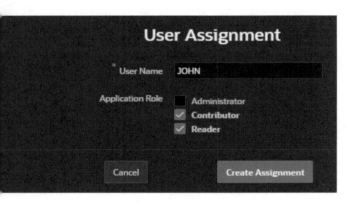

12. Before testing the module, grant contributor and reader rights to John for application access. Navigate to Shared Components page, then click the Application Access Control in the Security section. In the User Role Assignments section, click the Add User Role Assignment button. Enter JOHN in the User Name box and check both the Contributor and Reader roles. Click the Create Assignment button. Now, John can log in and access the application.

13. To test this module, open another browser, for example, Microsoft Edge and open the same application in it using John's credentials.

14. On the navigation bar, click the user's name (John) to expand the select list and choose the Settings option. In the Settings dialog box, click Off. This action will open another dialog. Check Enable push notifications on this device and close the dialog box. If you repeat this step, you will see that push notifications have been turned on for John.

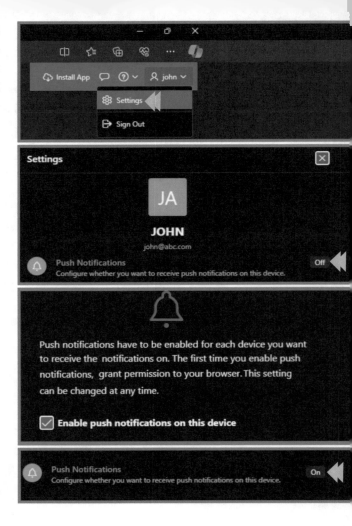

15. Open the two application sessions side-by-side. In the first session, logged in as the application administrator, complete the push notification form by entering JOHN in the user field, adding a title, and a message, and then click the Send button. After a brief wait, you will receive the notification in John's logged-in session. Connect to the application on your mobile device using John's credentials. The same notification will appear on the mobile device. Log out from the mobile device. Send another message to John, who is currently offline and not using the application. The notification will still appear on John's mobile device, even though he is offline.

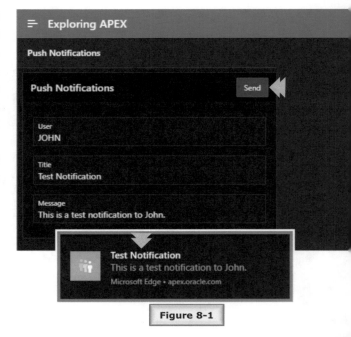

Figure 8-1

In this segment, you will discover the process of seamlessly incorporating maps into your Oracle APEX applications. Modern organizations have valuable spatial data in their databases – customer locations, competitors, shipments, and more. Oracle APEX's Map feature streamlines map creation and integration, empowering businesses to retrieve, analyze, and visualize spatial information.

Spatial data, often referred to as geospatial data, encompasses information tied to geographic details. It includes latitude and longitude coordinates defining precise Earth locations. Oracle APEX supports various spatial geometry objects like Points, Lines, Polygons, Heat Maps, and Extruded Polygons. Here, we focus on creating the Points spatial geometry object.

In this exercise, we'll utilize the Points object to generate a map visualizing the locations of educational units in the Chicago Public School District. The initial layer on the map features blue markers (A) that represent the location of each unit. Red markers (B) indicate specialty units. Specialty schools provide students with the opportunity to explore their interests and talents in a focused and supportive environment. The map retrieves its data from the 'Chicago_Schools' table that you will create in this section.

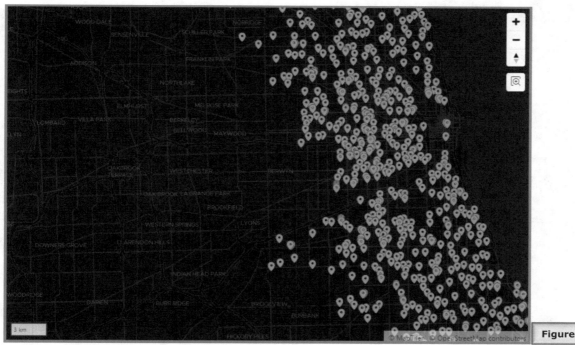

Figure 8-2

First, create the 'Chicago_Schools' table and populate it with data using the Data Workshop utility. The Data Workshop utility in Oracle APEX is a tool that allows you to load and unload data to and from a database. It can be used to import data from external sources, such as CSV files, XML files, and other databases. It can also be used to export data from the database to external sources. In this exercise, we will utilize the 'Chicago_Schools.csv' file, which is available in the book's source folder. This CSV file contains school information, including latitude (lat) and longitude (lng) columns, which form a grid system for pinpointing precise locations on the US map. Execute the steps below to create and populate the table:

1. In the main Oracle APEX menu, click the SQL Workshop. Then, select Data Workshop from the Utilities sub-menu.

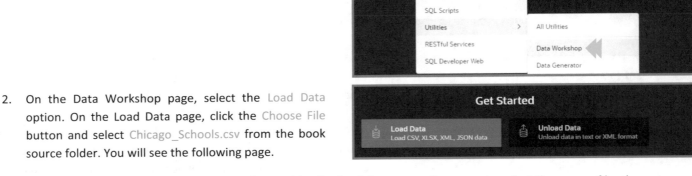

2. On the Data Workshop page, select the Load Data option. On the Load Data page, click the Choose File button and select Chicago_Schools.csv from the book source folder. You will see the following page.

This page is used to load data into a database table. The load data page allows you to select the source file, the table to load the data into, and the data types for each column in the source file.

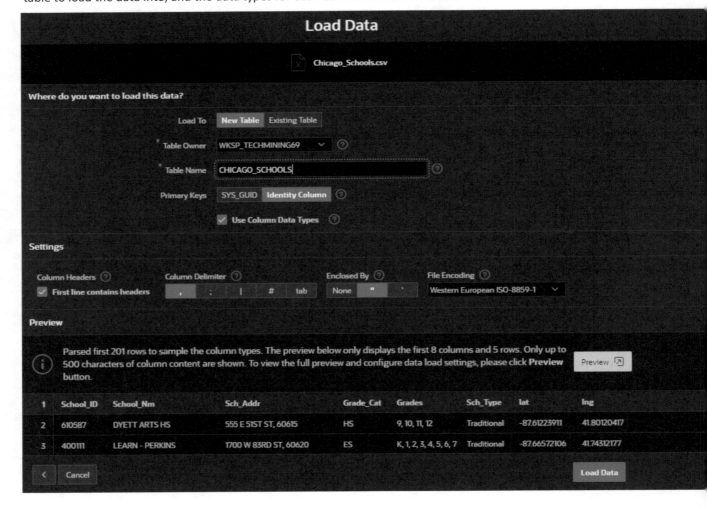

3. Select the New Table option for Load To. Enter CHICAGO_SCHOOLS for the new table name. Leaving all other options to their default values, click the Load Data button. You will see "Table CHICAGO_SCHOOLS created with 654 rows!" message. Click the View Table button to view the uploaded data in Object Browser.

The load data screen has the following main components:

Load To: This section allows you to select the table to load the data into.

New Table: This option creates a new table in the database to store the loaded data.

Existing Table: This option loads the data into an existing table in the database.

Table Name: This field specifies the name of the table to load the data into.

Table Owner: This field specifies the owner of the table to load the data into.

Primary Keys: This section allows you to specify the primary key columns for the table.

Identity Column: This option specifies the identity column for the table.

Use Column Data Types: This option loads the data into the table using the same data types as the source file.

Settings: This section allows you to configure the data loading process.

Column Headers: This option specifies whether the source file has column headers.

First line contains headers: This option specifies whether the first line of the source file contains column headers.

Column Delimiter: This option specifies the delimiter used to separate the columns in the source file.

Enclosed By: This option specifies the character used to enclose values in the source file.

File Encoding: This option specifies the encoding of the source file.

Preview: This section displays a preview of the first few lines of the source file.

Cancel: This button is used to cancel the data loading process.

Load Data: This button is used to start the data loading process.

4. Now, create a map page to visualize data from the Chicago Schools table. As usual, click the Create Page button and on the first Create Page wizard screen, select the Map option.

5. Fill in the page definitions as depicted in the adjacent figure and click Next.

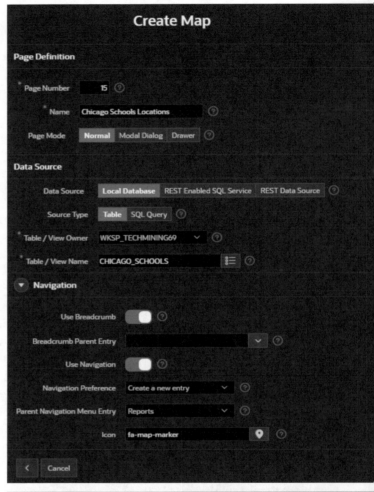

6. Select options on the next screen as illustrated in the adjacent figure. The Points option selected for the Map Style is used to store the coordinate location of a customer site, a store location, a delivery address, and so on. Spatial objects (also known as geometries) to be displayed on the map can be sourced from a Geometry Column or from Two Numeric Columns, containing longitude (LAT) and latitude (LNG) values. In this example, we are using the latter option because the Chicago Schools table contains these two columns. We also picked the School Name column. The value of this column will be displayed as a tooltip when the mouse pointer is hovered over a spatial geometry on the map. Click the Create Page button.

Run the page. Click the Zoom in icon on the map to view the locations.

Oracle APEX offers various types of maps and mapping features to cater to different needs and use cases within your applications. Here are some of the different types of maps and their typical usage in Oracle APEX:

Point Maps:
- Definition: A Point Map in Oracle APEX is a type of map used to display individual data points as markers on a geographical map. Each data point is represented by a marker or icon, making it easy to visualize the location of specific entities, such as addresses, places of interest, or events.
- Usage: Point maps are commonly used to showcase the geographic distribution of specific entities, such as store branches, customer locations, or event venues. Users can interact with the markers to access additional information about each point.

Heat Maps:
- Definition: A Heat Map in Oracle APEX is a map type that visually represents data density or concentration in a geographic area. Heat maps use color gradients to show the intensity of data values, with warmer colors (e.g., red) indicating higher data concentration and cooler colors (e.g., blue) representing lower data concentration.
- Usage: Heat maps are ideal for highlighting data trends and hotspots. They can be used to visualize patterns in data, such as website traffic density, the popularity of locations, or the concentration of events or incidents on a map. The intensity of the color indicates the data's significance within a specific area.

Lines Map:
- Definition: A Lines Map in Oracle APEX is a type of map that is used to display and visualize lines or paths on a geographic map. These lines often represent routes, connections, or journeys between different points on the map.
- Usage: Lines maps are suitable for displaying and tracking routes, such as flight paths, hiking trails, driving directions, and any other scenarios where you need to illustrate connections between locations. Users can follow the lines to understand the spatial relationships between points.

Polygons Map:
- Definition: A Polygons Map in Oracle APEX is designed to display and highlight specific geographic regions or areas on the map. These regions are typically defined by enclosing them with closed shapes, such as polygons.
- Usage: Polygons maps are commonly used to visualize regions like countries, states, counties, or any other defined areas. They are suitable for choropleth maps, where you can assign different colors to regions based on data values. This makes them useful for displaying data distribution across geographic areas.

Extruded Polygons Map:
- Definition: An Extruded Polygons Map in Oracle APEX is an advanced map type that not only displays geographic regions but also adds a third dimension by extruding these regions to represent height or volume.
- Usage: Extruded polygons are often used when you want to show the volume or magnitude of data within geographic regions. For example, you can use extruded polygons to display the population density of different regions by varying the height of polygons based on population data. This map type provides a unique way to visualize spatial data with depth and perspective.

The new Image Upload page item in Oracle APEX is a page item that allows users to upload images to an Oracle APEX application. This page item is based on the HTML5 File API, which provides a number of performance improvements over the previous image upload mechanism in Oracle APEX. The new Image Upload page item is more flexible and configurable than the previous image upload mechanism. You can use the new Image Upload page item to specify the maximum file size, allowed file types, crop and resize the uploaded image, and display a preview of the uploaded image.

The new Image Upload page item is also more flexible and configurable than the previous image upload mechanism. For example, you can use the new Image Upload page item to:

- Specify the maximum file size that can be uploaded
- Specify the allowed file types
- Crop and resize the uploaded image
- Display a preview of the uploaded image
- Store the uploaded image in the database or in a file system

To use the new Image Upload page item, you simply need to add it to a page and then configure the page item's properties. Once the page item is configured, you can test it by uploading an image to the application. It is a valuable addition to Oracle APEX. It provides a number of improvements over the previous image upload mechanism, including improved performance, increased flexibility, and enhanced security.

Here are some examples of how the new Image Upload page item can be used:

- To upload profile pictures for users of your application
- To upload product images for an e-commerce application
- To upload gallery images for a photo sharing application
- To upload document images for a file management application

QR CODE

The new QR Code page item in Oracle Apex allows developers to easily generate and display QR codes on their pages. The QR Code page item is very easy to use. You simply need to add it to a page and then configure its properties. This item dynamically encodes the selected source value into a QR code and displays it.

A QR code (Quick Response code) is a type of two-dimensional barcode that can be read easily by a camera. QR codes are often used to encode website URLs, product information, or other types of data. When scanned, a QR code can take the user to a specific web page, open a file, or perform another action.

QR codes are becoming increasingly popular because they are easy to use and can be used for a variety of purposes. For example, QR codes can be used to:

- Share contact information
- Promote products or services
- Provide directions
- Enable mobile payments
- Track inventory
- Authenticate users

QR codes can be created using a variety of online and offline tools. Once created, QR codes can be printed on paper, displayed on screens, or embedded in digital media.

To scan a QR code, users simply need to open a QR code scanning app on their smartphone or tablet and point the camera at the QR code. The scanning app will then decode the QR code and perform the appropriate action.

QR codes are a versatile and powerful tool that can be used for a variety of purposes. As QR code scanning technology continues to improve, we can expect to see QR codes used even more widely in the future.

Here are some examples of how QR codes are being used today:

- In retail: QR codes can be used to display product information, provide coupons, and enable mobile payments.
- In hospitality: QR codes can be used to check into hotels, order food and drinks, and access tourist information.
- In education: QR codes can be used to provide students with access to additional resources, such as videos, articles, and worksheets.
- In transportation: QR codes can be used to purchase tickets, board buses and trains, and access real-time travel information.
- In marketing: QR codes can be used to promote products and services, drive traffic to websites, and collect data from customers.

QR codes are a convenient and effective way to share information and perform actions. As QR code technology continues to evolve, we can expect to see QR codes used in even more innovative and exciting ways.

Let's dive and explore the functionality of the two new page items. To begin, create a new table named 'EMPLOYEES' and insert a single record into this table to use for testing the two new page items. You can find instructions on creating the new table in Chapter 3.

1. Here is the structure of the EMPLOYEES table. The most important property of the QR Code page item is Data Type where you select the type of the content that the QR code contains. A corresponding prefix value is inserted in front of the selected source value to affect how the user QR Code scanner will interact with the content.

   Available options include:
   a. Plain Text
   b. URL: The URL will open in a browser.
   c. Email: Compose a new email to an email address. The expected format of the email address is a valid email address without leading or trailing spaces.
   d. Geo location: Opens a map application to specific coordinates. The expected format of the input coordinates is lattitude,longitude with no leading or trailing spaces.

   We will create four QR Codes for EMPNAME, URL, EMAIL, and GEOLOCATION columns in this table and will use the new Image Upload page item to upload, crop and save images of employees.

EMPLOYEES

| Columns | Data | Indexes | Constraints | Grants | Statistics | Triggers |

+ Add Column   Modify Column   [A] Rename Column   Drop Column

Column Name	Data Type	Nullable	Default	Primary Key
EMPID	NUMBER	N	"WKSP_	1
EMPNAME	VARCHAR2(25 CHAR)	Y		
EMPIMAGE	BLOB	Y		
URL	VARCHAR2(100 CHAR)	Y		
EMAIL	VARCHAR2(25 CHAR)	Y		
GEOLOCATION	VARCHAR2(16 CHAR)	Y		

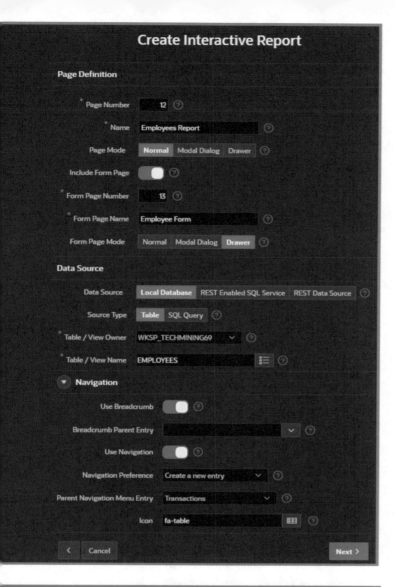

Create Interactive Report

Page Definition

* Page Number   12 ⑦

* Name   Employees Report ⑦

Page Mode   [Normal] Modal Dialog Drawer ⑦

Include Form Page   ⬤ ⑦

* Form Page Number   13 ⑦

* Form Page Name   Employee Form ⑦

Form Page Mode   Normal Modal Dialog [Drawer] ⑦

Data Source

Data Source   [Local Database] REST Enabled SQL Service REST Data Source ⑦

Source Type   [Table] SQL Query ⑦

* Table / View Owner   WKSP_TECHMINING69 ∨ ⑦

* Table / View Name   EMPLOYEES ☰ ⑦

▼ **Navigation**

Use Breadcrumb   ⬤ ⑦

Breadcrumb Parent Entry   ∨ ⑦

Use Navigation   ⬤ ⑦

Navigation Preference   Create a new entry ∨ ⑦

Parent Navigation Menu Entry   Transactions ∨ ⑦

Icon   fa-table ⊞ ⑦

‹ Cancel   Next ›

---

2. Create interactive report and form pages using the attributes depicted in the adjacent figure and click Next. On the subsequent wizard screen, select EMPID as the primary key and create the two pages.

   For this exercise, we selected Drawer for Form Page Mode attribute. The Drawer form page mode in Oracle Apex is a new feature that allows you to create forms that slide out from the side of the page. This can be useful for creating forms that are not essential to the main content of the page, such as login forms, search forms, and contact forms.

3. Open the form page (Page 13) in page designer. Click on the image page item (P13_EMPIMAGE). Change its type from File Upload to the new Image Upload page item. Select Large for Preview Size in the Display section to set the size of the displayed preview. In the Cropping section, enable Allow Cropping and set Aspect Ratio to 1:1 (square). By enabling cropping, you specify that users can crop uploaded images. When enabled you will also be able to set the aspect ratio for the cropped image. By default, the aspect ratio will match the file being uploaded unless another option is defined. Save the page.

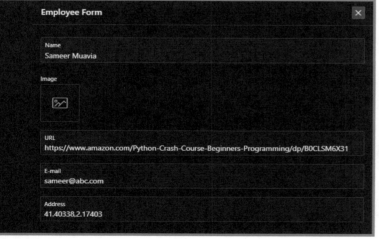

Employee Form   ✕

Name
Sameer Muavia

Image
🖼️

URL
https://www.amazon.com/Python-Crash-Course-Beginners-Programming/dp/B0CLSM6X31

E-mail
sameer@abc.com

Address
41.40338,2.17403

---

4. Run the report page (Page 13) and click Create to add a new record. Fill in the form using the values provided in the following table:

FIELD	VALUE
Name	Sameer Muavia
URL	https://www.amazon.com/Python-Crash-Course-Beginners-Programming/dp/B0CLSM6X31
E-mail	sameer@abc.com
Address	41.40338,2.17403

5. Click the image icon in the Image field. Select employees.jpg file, which is available in the book code. Drag the image file and select the image to crop. Use the slider to zoom the image. After the adjustment, click Apply. The image will appear on the form. Click Create to save this record.

6. On the Rendering tab on Page 13, press and hold the control key on your keyboard and click the page items P13_EMPNAME, P13_URL, P13_EMAIL, and P13_GEOLOCATION to select these four page items. In the Property Editor, change the Type property from Text Field to QR Code. This action will change the type of all the selected page items simultaneously. Save the page and call it from the report page by editing the employee record you just entered. Observe that all the four-page items have been transformed into QR Codes.

7. Install a QR Code scanner app from the app store on your mobile device and scan each of these codes individually. The results of scanning these QR codes are illustrated in the following screenshots.

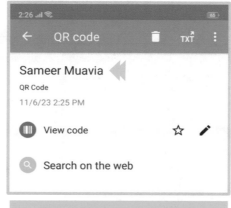

Output of the Name QR Code.

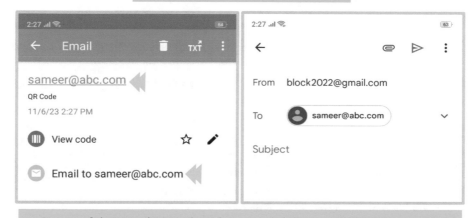

Output of the E-mail QR Code. When you click the email address, an email client will appear on your mobile device to compose a new email and send it to the employee.

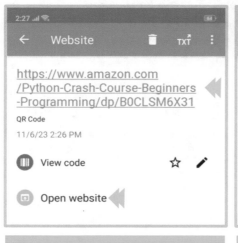

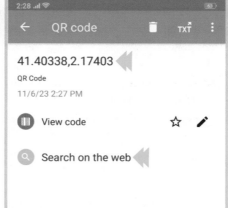

Scanning the URL QR Code will render the saved URL. Clicking the URL will take you to the Amazon website.

The address QR Code will display the latitude and longitude values. Clicking the "Search on the web" link will open the location in a map.

WHAT YOU LEARNED

In this chapter, we explored the powerful features and capabilities of Oracle APEX related to Progressive Web Applications (PWAs), Push Notifications, and Maps. These modern web technologies enhance the user experience and provide dynamic, interactive functionalities within APEX applications.

Progressive Web Applications (PWAs):
- We delved into the world of PWAs, which are web applications that offer the performance and capabilities of native desktop applications.
- The chapter explained how to enable the PWA feature during application creation or for existing applications.
- We discussed the options for enabling offline support, push notifications, and customizing the display and behavior of PWAs.

Push Notifications:
- Push notifications were introduced as a vital feature of PWAs, allowing applications to send real-time alerts and updates to users.
- We explored how to configure push notifications in Oracle APEX applications and send messages to users even when the application is not open.

Maps in Oracle APEX:
- The chapter covered different types of maps available in APEX, including Point Maps, Heat Maps, Lines Maps, Polygons Maps, Extruded Polygons Maps, and more.
- We learned how to create interactive and data-driven maps by creating a Points map.
- Data visualization and geographic representation were discussed as key applications of maps in APEX.

Image Upload and QR Code:
- We also went through a couple of new page items in Oracle APEX - Image Upload and QR Code. These page items provide developers with easy-to-use and powerful tools for adding image upload and QR code functionality to their applications. The Image Upload page item allows users to upload images to an Oracle Apex application, while the QR Code page item allows developers to easily generate and display QR codes on their pages.

In this chapter, you gained a comprehensive understanding of how to harness the potential of PWAs, push notifications, maps, Image Upload, and QR Code in Oracle APEX applications. These technologies enhance the user experience, extend the functionality of web applications, and provide dynamic ways to interact with geographic and location-based data.

9

SECURITY IN

ORACLE APEX

Security in Oracle APEX is the process of protecting applications and data from unauthorized access, use, disclosure, disruption, modification, or destruction. Oracle APEX provides a variety of security features that can be used to implement a comprehensive security strategy. Authentication and authorization are two crucial aspects of security in Oracle APEX that control access to APEX applications. Here's an overview of each:

AUTHENTICATION

Authentication is the process of verifying the identity of a user or system trying to access an APEX application. APEX supports various authentication methods to authenticate users:

Database Authentication

Users are authenticated against a database user account. They enter their database username and password to access the application. This method is often used for internal applications where users have database accounts.

LDAP Authentication

Oracle APEX can be configured to use LDAP (Lightweight Directory Access Protocol) to authenticate users. LDAP is commonly used in organizations with centralized user directories, such as Active Directory.

Single Sign-On & OAuth

Single Sign-On (SSO) and OAuth APEX can integrate with various single sign-on solutions, enabling users to log in once and access multiple applications without re-entering credentials. OAuth is used for allowing third-party applications to access APEX resources securely.

Social Sign-In

Users can log in using their social media accounts, such as Google or Facebook. APEX integrates with OAuth to enable social sign-in.

Custom Authentication

Developers can create custom authentication schemes to implement authentication methods tailored to specific needs. This is useful when standard methods do not suffice.

AUTHORIZATION

Authorization, on the other hand, determines what actions or resources a user is allowed to access once they are authenticated. It defines permissions and privileges for various application components:

Roles

Oracle APEX uses roles to manage user access. Developers create roles and assign them to users. Each role has a set of privileges, such as accessing specific pages, reports, or application components.

Page-Level Authorization

Developers can specify which roles are allowed to access individual pages within an application. This fine-grained control helps ensure that only authorized users can view or modify specific pages.

Component-Level

Beyond pages, you can also control access at the component level. This is called Component-Level Authorization. For instance, you can set conditions that determine whether a button or report is visible to a user based on their role.

Authorization Schemes

Developers can define custom logic for determining whether a user is authorized to access specific application components. Authorization schemes are powerful tools for implementing complex access control rules.

Data Security

Oracle APEX allows for data security policies, ensuring that users can only view or manipulate data they have permission to access. This is crucial for applications with sensitive data.

In summary, authentication verifies a user's identity, while authorization controls what actions they can perform within an APEX application. Effective use of these security features is essential for protecting your application and ensuring that users can access the right resources based on their roles and permissions.

ADMINISTRATION IN APEX

Oracle APEX includes two distinct types of administrators: Workspace administrators and Instance administrators. A workspace administrator primarily oversees administrative tasks related to a specific workspace. These responsibilities encompass user account management, workspace activity monitoring, and log file access. Conversely, instance administrators are responsible for the comprehensive management of the entire Oracle APEX instance. In the context of this book, you will assume the role of a workspace administrator, as it is a hosted environment where the instance administrator role is not accessible, with such duties being handled by the Oracle APEX team.

The role of a Workspace Administrator in Oracle APEX is to manage and oversee administrative activities within a specific workspace. Workspaces in APEX provide a logical separation of applications and users, allowing different teams or projects to work independently within the same APEX instance. Workspace Administrators have the following responsibilities:

User Management

- Create, manage, and delete user accounts within the workspace.
- Define user roles and assign roles to users to control their privileges and access rights within the workspace.

Application Management

- Create and maintain APEX applications within the workspace.
- Control access to applications by specifying which users or roles can view, edit, or run specific applications.

Security & Access Control

- Implement and manage access control and data security within applications.
- Set up page-level and component-level authorization to restrict user access based on roles and privileges.

Monitoring & Reporting

- Monitor workspace activities, including application usage, user logins, and application performance.
- Generate reports and view log files to track and troubleshoot issues within the workspace.

Workspace Configuration

- Configure workspace-level settings, such as email settings, feedback preferences, and notifications.
- Define security policies and other global settings that apply to applications within the workspace.

Workspace Administration

- Manage workspace attributes, including the workspace name, description, and logo.
- Control the appearance and behavior of the workspace, including themes, templates, and authentication options.

Collaboration

- Collaborate with application developers, contributors, and readers to ensure that applications are developed and used effectively.
- Provide support and guidance to users and teams working within the workspace.

Backup & Recovery

- Establish and execute backup and recovery procedures for applications and workspace data to prevent data loss.

General Maintenance

- Perform routine maintenance tasks, such as purging old data, optimizing application performance, and ensuring that workspace resources are used efficiently.

Workspace Administrators play a critical role in managing and maintaining a specific workspace, ensuring that applications are secure, accessible, and function as intended. They act as the point of contact for users within the workspace and are responsible for configuring the workspace's settings to align with the goals and requirements of the projects or teams working within it.

When you enable the "Access Control" feature during the creation of a new Oracle APEX application (see Chapter 2), the APEX engine generates default entries for Authentication Schemes, Authorization Schemes, and Application Access Control. These entries provide a foundational framework for managing access control and security within your application.

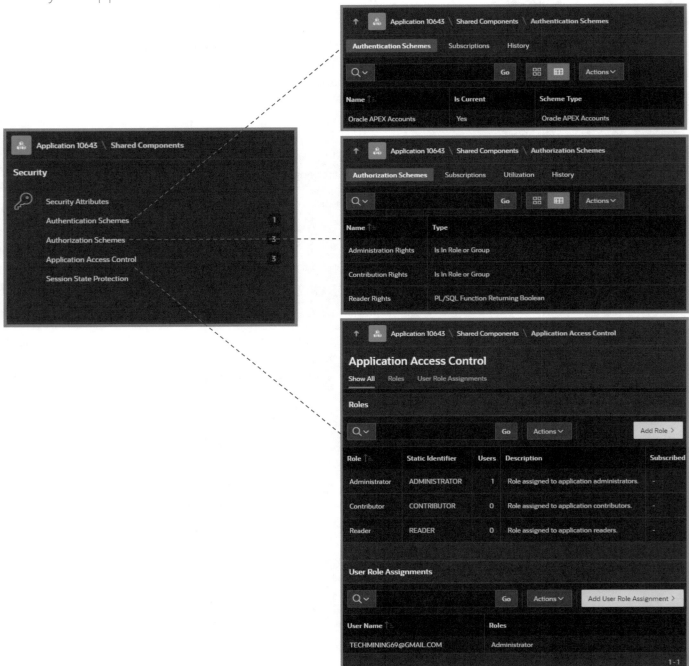

Here's a definition for each of the default entries that are created when you enable the "Access Control" feature during the creation of a new Oracle APEX application:

Authentication Scheme: Oracle APEX Accounts:
- Definition: The "Oracle APEX Accounts" authentication scheme is a default authentication scheme that enables users to log in to the application using credentials stored in the APEX database. It validates user identities and allows access to the application based on username and password.
- Purpose: This authentication scheme is used to authenticate and verify users when they log in to the APEX application. Users must provide valid credentials to access the application.

Authorization Scheme: Administration Rights:
- Definition: The "Administration Rights" authorization scheme is a default authorization scheme that specifies which users or roles have administrator-level privileges within the application. Users assigned to this authorization scheme typically have full access to all administrative functions and settings of the application.
- Purpose: This authorization scheme is used to define and control who can perform administrative tasks within the application, such as managing user accounts, configuring application settings, and accessing sensitive administrative areas.

Authorization Scheme: Contribution Rights:
- Definition: The "Contribution Rights" authorization scheme is a default authorization scheme that determines which users or roles have the privilege to edit and contribute to the application. Users assigned to this authorization scheme can modify and update application data and components.
- Purpose: This authorization scheme is used to restrict access to certain areas of the application where users can edit and contribute to the content. It is commonly applied to areas where data can be modified.

Authorization Scheme: Reader Rights:
- Definition: The "Reader Rights" authorization scheme is a default authorization scheme that controls which users or roles have read-only access to the application. Users assigned to this authorization scheme can view the application but are not allowed to make changes.
- Purpose: This authorization scheme is employed to grant access to users who need to view and interact with the application but should not have editing or contributing privileges. It ensures that certain areas of the application are read-only for the users assigned to this scheme.

Roles: Administrator, Contributor, Reader:
- Administrator Role: Users assigned to the "Administrator" role have full administrative control over the application. They can manage user accounts, configure application settings, and access all administrative functions.
- Contributor Role: Users assigned to the "Contributor" role have edit and contribution privileges within the application. They can modify and update application data and components but do not have administrative control.
- Reader Role: Users assigned to the "Reader" role have read-only access to the application. They can view and interact with the application's content but are restricted from making changes.

These default entries provide a foundational framework for access control within the application. You can further customize and extend these entries based on your application's specific requirements to ensure that users have the appropriate level of access and security.

Let's walk through a simple scenario to understand the roles of Contributor and Reader. The diagram below illustrates the security structure you will implement in your application.

On the left, we have the user David, who has the Contributor role. We have assigned the 'Contribution Rights' authorization scheme to the 'Create' button on the 'Students Report' page (Page 3). Because David has the Contributor role, and the 'Create' button is associated with the 'Contribution Rights' authorization scheme, the button is visible on the page for this user. In other words, administrators and contributors have the ability to create new students.

On the right side, we present a different scenario with the user ADAM, who has been granted the Reader role. When ADAM attempts to access the same report page, the 'Create' button is not displayed. This is because the button is linked to the 'Contribution Rights' authorization scheme.

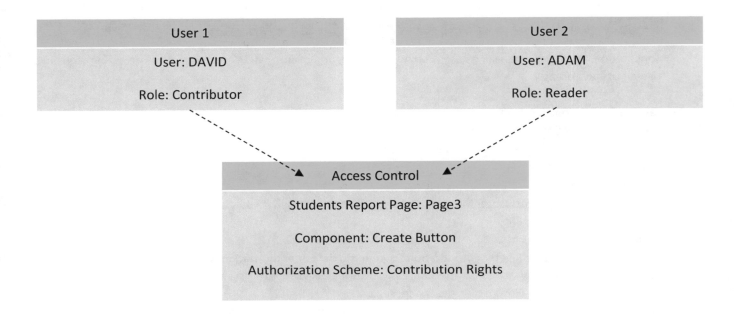

Execute the following steps to create the two users and to test the application access control scenario depicted in the figure above.

1. Click the Administration icon and then click the Manage Users and Groups option. On the Manage Users and Groups page, click the Users tab. Click the Create User button. On the Create User page, enter a username (for example, DAVID). Type the user's email address (for example, david@abcglobal.com). Scroll down to the Password section. Enter and confirm case sensitive user's password. Click the Create User button. Repeat this step to create Adam's account. The two users will be added to the users list.

   Run the application and attempt to log in using David's credentials. You will receive an 'Access denied by Application security check' message. This message is displayed because the user has not been granted access to the application. Proceed to the next steps to grant application access privileges to this user.

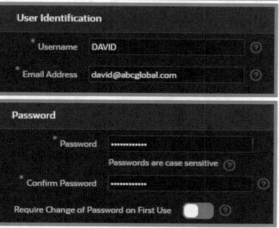

2. On the error page, click the OK button to access the login page again. Enter your workspace administrator credentials to log in. Click the Administration option in the application menu, and then click the Add User button in the Access Control pane to your right.

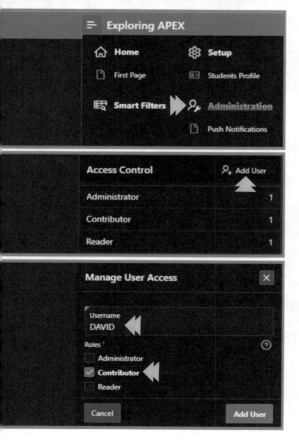

3. On the Manage User Access page, enter DAVID in the Username box, and grant him the Contributor role. Click the Add User button. Repat these instructions for Adam and grant him the Reader role only.

   Log out and log back in using David's credentials. This time, you will be granted access to the application. Note that the Administration menu will not be displayed for these users, as they do not have administrator privileges.

In the following set of steps, you will implement the Contribution Rights authorization scheme to test access to page, page components, and application menu. You now have three application users – you (workspace administrator), David (Contributor), and Adam (Reader).

1. Open Page 3 in Page Designer. On the Rendering tab to your left, click the Create button to select it. In the Properties pane, set Authorization Scheme (in the Security section) to Contribution Rights, and save the change. The button is now associated with the selected authorization scheme.

   Run the application using David's credentials. Select Students Profile from the Setup menu. The Create button should be visible for David, because he possesses the contributor role.

   Log out and log back in using Adam's credentials. Once again, select the Students Profile option from the Setup menu. On this occasion, the Create button will not be rendered, because the user has the Reader role – that is, he cannot create new students.

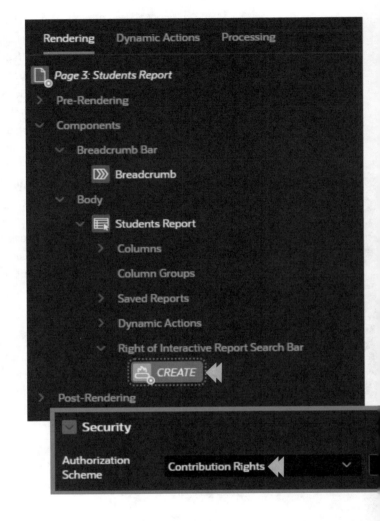

2. After testing page component access control, let's see how to restrict user from accessing an application page. Switch back to the designer interface. Click the root node - Page 3: Students Report. In the Properties pane, scroll down to the Security section, and set Authorization Scheme to Contribution Rights. Save and run the page. This time the page itself will not be rendered and you will see a message "Insufficient privileges, user is not a Contributor" instead. Log in as David and observe that both page and the Create button are rendered to David.

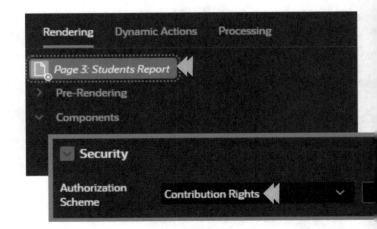

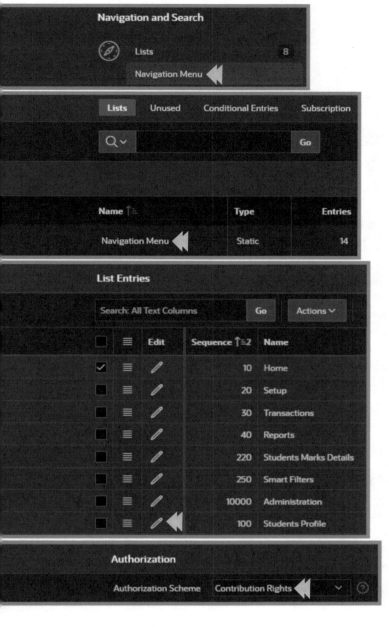

3. Finally, let's check out the application menu access. Go to Shared Components interface, and select Navigation Menu followed by the Navigation Menu option. Click the edit link representing Students Profile menu entry. On the List Entry page, scroll down to the Authorization Scheme section and set it to Contribution Rights, and click the Apply Changes button. Switch to the application tab in your browser, and refresh the Students Report page. The application menu should still be listing the Students Profile entry for David. Sign out and log in as Adam. There you go! The Students Profile entry from the Setup menu has vanished. So, this step demonstrated how to protect application menu options from unauthorized people.

WHAT YOU LEARNED

Security in Oracle APEX refers to the measures, practices, and tools used to protect APEX applications and their data from unauthorized access, misuse, and threats. It encompasses various aspects of safeguarding an application's confidentiality, integrity, and availability. Key components of security in APEX include:

- **Authentication:** The process of verifying the identity of users or systems accessing an APEX application. APEX supports different authentication methods, such as database authentication, LDAP, SSO, OAuth, and custom authentication schemes.
- **Authorization:** Determining what actions or resources authenticated users can access within an application. This involves defining roles, privileges, page-level authorization, component-level authorization, and authorization schemes.
- **Data Security:** Ensuring that users can only view or modify data they have permission to access. Data security policies are applied to restrict data visibility and manipulation based on user roles and attributes.
- **Encryption:** Protecting sensitive data by encrypting it both in transit and at rest. APEX applications often use HTTPS for secure communication and allow encryption of database columns using Transparent Data Encryption (TDE).
- **Cross-Site Scripting (XSS) Prevention:** Implementing measures to prevent XSS attacks, which can compromise an application's security. APEX provides built-in safeguards, and developers should follow best practices to avoid XSS vulnerabilities.
- **SQL Injection Prevention:** Guarding against SQL injection attacks by using bind variables, proper escaping, and input validation to ensure that user inputs do not pose a risk to the application's database.
- **Security Patching:** Keeping the APEX environment and underlying database up to date with security patches and updates to protect against known vulnerabilities.
- **Backup and Recovery:** Establishing a robust backup and recovery strategy to ensure data can be restored in the event of data loss or security breaches.
- **Session Management:** Managing user sessions securely, including mechanisms for session timeout, password policies, and prevention of session fixation attacks.
- **Auditing and Logging:** Recording and monitoring application activities, including login attempts, access to sensitive data, and administrative actions. This helps in identifying and responding to security incidents.
- **Access Control:** Ensuring that administrative functions, sensitive data, and system configurations are accessible only to authorized users and administrators.
- **User Training:** Educating users and administrators about security best practices, such as password policies, safe data handling, and recognizing security threats like phishing.
- **Compliance:** Ensuring that the application complies with relevant security standards and regulations, such as GDPR, HIPAA, or industry-specific security requirements.
- **Testing and Vulnerability Scanning:** Conducting regular security assessments, penetration testing, and vulnerability scans to identify and address potential security weaknesses.

Security in APEX is an ongoing process that requires a combination of proper design, development practices, and vigilant monitoring to mitigate risks and protect against security threats. It is essential to incorporate security considerations from the inception of application design and to continually update and enhance security measures as the application evolves.

10

APPLICATION

DEPLOYMENT

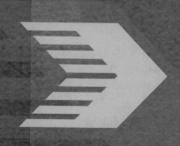

Application deployment in Oracle APEX refers to the process of making an APEX application available for users to access and use. This involves moving an application from a development environment to a production environment where it can be accessed by end-users. Here are the steps involved in the application deployment process in Oracle APEX:

1. Export Application

In the Oracle APEX development environment, start by exporting your application. This creates a file (usually with a .sql extension) that contains all the application's components, configurations, and metadata.

2. Transfer Files

Transfer the exported application file to your production environment. This can be done through file transfer protocols, cloud storage, or other means.

3. Import Application

In the production environment, use Oracle APEX to import the application. This is typically done through the APEX Application Builder interface.

4. Database Synchronization

Ensure that the database objects (tables, views, packages, etc.) required for the application are available in the production database. If there are any differences between the development and production databases, make the necessary adjustments.

5. Set Up Web Server

Configure your web server or hosting environment to serve the application. This may involve setting up a web server, configuring domain names, and obtaining SSL certificates for secure access.

6. Security Configuration

Review and configure security settings for the production environment. This includes user authentication, authorization, and securing access to sensitive data.

7. User Training

Train end-users and administrators on how to use the application effectively and handle common tasks.

8. Monitoring and Maintenance

Set up monitoring tools and establish a maintenance plan to ensure the ongoing health and performance of the application.

9. Go Live

Once you are confident in the stability of the application in the production environment, make the application accessible to end-users. This is often referred to as "going live" or "launching" the application.

10. Post-Deployment Support

Provide post-deployment support to address any issues that may arise and to make necessary updates and improvements.

Application deployment in Oracle APEX is a critical phase in the software development lifecycle, and proper planning and execution are essential to ensure a smooth transition from development to production. It's important to follow best practices, have a rollback plan in case of issues, and communicate the deployment schedule to relevant stakeholders.

EXPORT APPLICATION

For the sake of simplicity, we will deploy the application within the same workspace to illustrate the deployment concept. This method is also relevant to a production environment. This section will illustrate the process of exporting an Oracle APEX application that can be imported into either a new workspace or the same one.

1. Sign in to Oracle APEX and edit the application.

2. On the App Builder page, click the Export/Import icon.

3. On the ensuing page, click the Export icon.

4. On the Export Application page, accept all the default values, and click the Export button. A file with a .sql extension will be saved in the Download folder or another folder specified in your browser. In my case, the name of this file is 'f250373.sql,' representing my application ID.

EXPORT/IMPORT DATA

When you deploy an Oracle APEX application, you might need to transfer database objects along with the application to ensure that the application works correctly in the production environment. Here are the general steps to transfer database objects along with your APEX application:

If your application relies on data, you'll need to migrate database objects like tables, views, sequences, and packages from the development environment to the production environment. This can be done using Data Pump, SQL scripts, or other ETL (Extract, Transform, Load) processes.

Data Pump (expdp/impdp)

Oracle Data Pump, often referred to as expdp (export data pump) and impdp (import data pump), is a set of utilities in Oracle Database used for high-speed and efficient transfer of data and metadata between databases. It is a powerful tool for backup, restore, and data migration tasks.

SQL Scripts

Create SQL scripts to recreate database objects in the production database. These scripts should include the necessary CREATE statements for tables, views, indexes, triggers, and other objects.

Database Links

If your production database is separate from the development database, you can use database links to access and migrate data from one database to another. To use database links to transfer data, you will need to create a database link on the development database that points to the production database. You can then use SQL statements to access and migrate data from the production database to the development database.

The specific steps and methods for migrating database objects will depend on your database system, your organization's procedures, and the complexity of your APEX application. Always follow best practices, maintain backups, and consider the specific needs of your project.

IMPORT APPLICATION

In Oracle Application Express (APEX), the "Import Application" process is a feature that allows you to import an APEX application definition from an exported application file (with a .sql extension). This process is used to bring in an application, including its components, pages, and related objects, from one environment (e.g., development) to another (e.g., production). Here are the steps to import the application using the exported file (f250373.sql) into the existing workspace you are connected to.

1. Sign in to Oracle APEX and click the App Builder icon.

2. On the App Builder page, click the Import icon.

3. On the Import screen, click the Drag and Drop area and select the exported file (f250373.sql). For the File Type option, select Application, Page or Component Export, and click Next.

When you use the "Import Application" process, you typically have the option to specify the file type of the application export file you want to import. The option we selected here can be used to import:

Application: The "Application" option means you are importing a full application export file. This file contains the entire application definition, including all its components, pages, theme settings, shared components, and application-level attributes. When you import an "Application" export file, you are essentially bringing in the entire application and all its configurations into the target environment.

Page: The "Page" option indicates that you are importing a page-level export file. In this case, the export file only contains the definition of a single page within an application. This option is useful when you want to import or update specific pages from one application into another without affecting the rest of the application.

Component: The "Component" option allows you to import a specific component-level export file. APEX components can include items, regions, dynamic actions, and other individual elements that can be reused across applications. When you select this option, you are importing the definition of a single component into your application.

4. On the Install Application page, select the default value for Parsing Schema. Select Run and Build Application for Build Status. Select Auto Assign New Application ID option for Install As Application, and click the Install Application button. After a short while, the application will be installed with a new ID, and you can give it a test run.

Click the Run Application button. You may encounter an error message stating: "You are not authorized to view this application, either because you have not been granted access, or your account has been locked. Please contact the application administrator." This error occurs because application users are not exported as part of your application. When you deploy your application, you need to manually manage user-to-role assignments. Roles are exported as part of an application export and imported with application imports. Follow the steps below to address this error.

5. Edit the new application. Go to Shared Components, and click Application Access Control in the Security section. Using the Add User Role Assignment button add the three users as shown in the following figure. Now you can access the application using the same credentials of these users.

SECURING APPLICATION

At this stage, Adam can use the Developers Toolbar to access the application source and change his status. In this exercise, we are going to prevent users from modifying the application by suppressing the toolbar.

1. Edit the new application.

2. Go to Shared Components page.

3. Click the Globalization Attributes link (under Globalization section).

4. Click the Definition tab.

5. Click the Availability sub-tab, set Build Status to Run Application Only, and click Apply Changes. Now, go to the App Builder interface and observe that the new application doesn't have the 'Edit' link. Click the 'Run' button, provide your sign-in credentials, and note that the Developer Toolbar has disappeared as well.

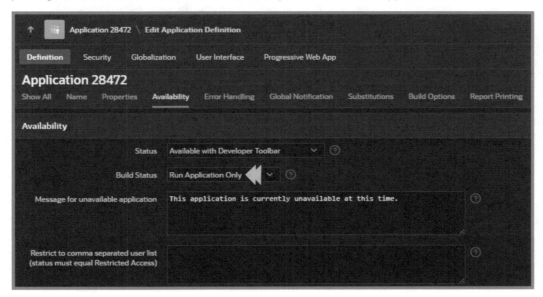

To make the application editable again, select App Builder | Workspace Utilities | All Workspace Utilities. On the Workspace Utilities page, select Build and App Status from the right sidebar. On Build Status and Application Status page, click the ID of the new application in the first report column, change the Build Status to Run and Build Application, and apply the change.

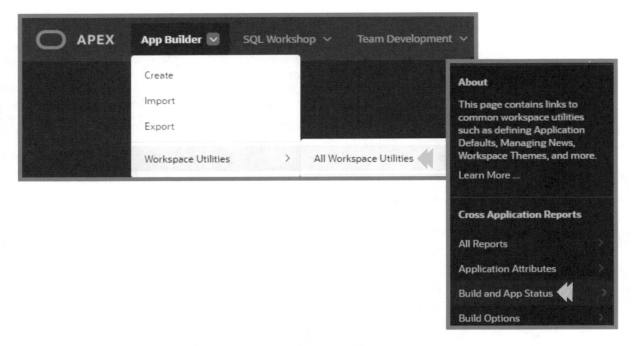

Congratulations, you have now successfully deployed your application within the same workspace. This deployment process ensures that your application is ready for use. The good news is that the same procedure can be applied to deploy your application to different environments or workspaces. Whether you're moving your application from a development environment to a production environment or sharing it with others, this process remains consistent and efficient. Your application is now ready to be accessed, tested, and used according to your specific requirements.

DATA PACKAGER

You can effortlessly transfer your applications from one instance to another while also including data from specific tables using Data Packager. In this utility, you define the tables from which data is exported along with the application. Here are the steps to utilize this feature:

1. Open your application and click the Supporting Objects option on the App Builder page.

2. Click on the Installation Scripts option.

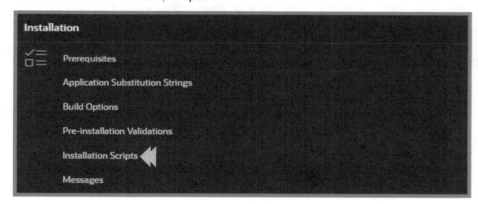

3. Click the Create button to create a new script. Then, click the icon labeled Create from Database Objects.

4. On the Create Script page, enter a name for the script - for example, Tables.sql. In Object Type, select TABLE and click Next.

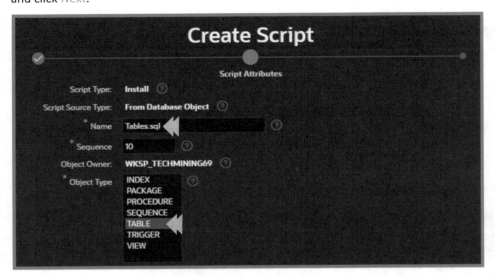

5. On the final Define Script wizard screen, move the tables you want for your application to the right pane, and click Next. The next screen will show the auto generated DDL statements that will create the selected tables. Click Create to complete this process.

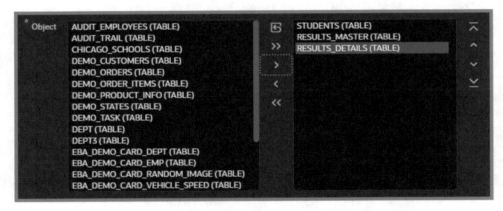

In the previous steps, we generated scripts for essential supporting objects required to package the application for installation in a different environment. To also migrate data alongside the application, Oracle APEX offers the Data Packager feature. Here are the steps to incorporate your data:

1. Once again, click the Create button on the Scripts page. On the Create Script page, click the Data Package option.

2. Enter a name for this script - for example, Data.sql. Move the required tables to the right pane and complete the wizard as usual. Note that BLOB data type is currently not supported for export in Data Package. So, the images have to be added manually to the STUDENTS table.

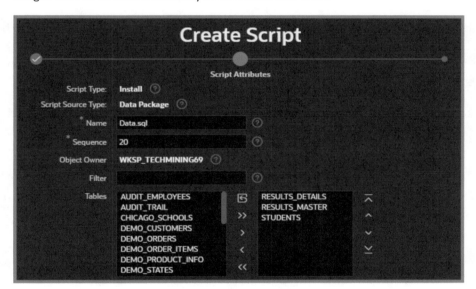

Two data package scripts will be created and added to shared components. Now that you have both the application and the underlying data packaged, you can export this application using the same procedure described in the 'Export Application' section earlier in this chapter. On the final wizard screen, select Yes and Install on Import Automatically for Supporting Object Definitions, and then click the Export button.

Now log into another workspace and import the exported application using the same process described in the "Import Application" section earlier. After completing the import process, navigate to Object Browser and review the application tables that are installed along with the underlying data.

WHAT YOU LEARNED

In this chapter, you learned how to deploying applications efficiently. It covered the following key topics:

- Export Application: The chapter begins by explaining the process of exporting an APEX application. Users are provided with a step-by-step guide on how to export their applications, making them ready for deployment to other environments.

- Export/Import Data: This section delves into the various options available for exporting and importing data along with APEX applications. It highlights the flexibility of the export/import process, making it suitable for a range of scenarios.

- Import Application: The chapter also discusses the import process, guiding users on how to import applications into their target environments. This complements the export process, ensuring a seamless transfer of applications.

- Securing Application: A crucial aspect of application deployment is security. The chapter covers how to enhance application security by changing the build status to "Run Application Only." This is essential for restricting unauthorized access during deployment.

- Data Packager: Another valuable tool explored in this chapter is the Data Packager. It details how to use this feature to create DDL (Data Definition Language) and DML (Data Manipulation Language) scripts for exporting both the application and associated database objects and data. This ensures a comprehensive and consistent transfer of all application components.

The chapter equipped you with the knowledge and skills needed to export, import, secure, and package your applications effectively, facilitating a smooth deployment process in various environments.

Dear Readers,

Thank you for choosing to read my book on Oracle APEX. I hope you find the content insightful and that it aids you in your journey to master this powerful development platform.

I hope you gained a solid understanding of Oracle APEX and its various features. However, I believe that learning should be an ongoing process, and there's always room to explore more advanced topics and real-world implementations.

That's why I'm excited to introduce my YouTube channel, where you can find a treasure trove of additional content that complements the book's teachings. On my channel, I cover a wide range of Oracle APEX topics, from beginner-level tutorials to advanced techniques that can take your skills to the next level.

Here's what you can expect from my YouTube channel:

1. Bonus Content: I've created exclusive videos related to the book's topics that delve deeper into specific concepts. These videos provide hands-on examples and practical demonstrations that reinforce the knowledge you've gained from the book.

2. Case Studies: Watch real-world case studies and learn how Oracle APEX is used to build powerful applications across different industries. Gain insights into best practices and discover how to tackle complex scenarios.

3. Community Interaction: The YouTube channel is a thriving community of like-minded Oracle APEX enthusiasts. By subscribing and engaging with the content, you'll have the opportunity to interact with fellow learners and exchange ideas.

4. Regular Updates: I regularly upload new videos to keep you updated on the latest features, tips, and tricks in Oracle APEX. There will always be something new for you to learn and implement in your projects.

To get started, visit **https://www.youtube.com/@TechMining69** and hit the subscribe button. By subscribing to the channel, you'll receive notifications whenever I upload new content, ensuring that you stay ahead in your Oracle APEX journey.

I encourage you to actively participate by leaving comments, asking questions, and sharing your thoughts on the videos. Your feedback and engagement are invaluable in shaping the content and ensuring that it addresses your specific needs and interests.

Thank you for being a part of this exciting learning journey. I look forward to seeing you on my YouTube channel, where we can continue exploring the endless possibilities of Oracle APEX together.

Happy learning!

Sa'ad Muavia

INDEX